MW01119313

Supernatural Power

John Koerner

Bloomington, IN  Milton Keynes, UK

authorHOUSE®

AuthorHouse™
1663 Liberty Drive, Suite 200
Bloomington, IN 47403
www.authorhouse.com
Phone: 1-800-839-8640

AuthorHouse™ UK Ltd.
500 Avebury Boulevard
Central Milton Keynes, MK9 2BE
www.authorhouse.co.uk
Phone: 08001974150

© 2007 John Koerner. All rights reserved.

No part of this book may be reproduced, stored in a retrieval system, or transmitted by any means without the written permission of the author.

First published by AuthorHouse 3/5/2007

ISBN: 978-1-4259-9061-9 (sc)

Library of Congress Control Number: 2007900360

Printed in the United States of America
Bloomington, Indiana

This book is printed on acid-free paper.

Dedicated again to the memory of
Anthony P. Losi
and
Salvatore L. Losi,
two other men of power.

Supernatural Power: Table of Contents

Introduction

Ever since Jesus turned water into wine, the Christian world has been fascinated by the subject of miracles, and in turn the men and women said to perform them. The topic speaks both to our humanity, and to our divinity, as people seek healing of their physical bodies through divinely guided human hands. To study the miraculous though is also at its core a quest for understanding, part of an insatiable desire to know the unknown.

In October and November, 1929, nearly a million people converged on one site in Massachusetts to participate in that very quest, for it seemed for a time that literally anything was possible. The lame walked, the sick were cured, the blind could see. The place was Holy Cross Cemetery in Malden, Massachusetts. The human being said to be responsible for these miraculous acts was a man named Father Patrick Joseph Power. He had been dead and buried there for six decades.

For several weeks until the cemetery gates were finally closed, scores of individuals claimed to be healed by this man. Yet who was this Father Patrick Power? What evidence is there to support that he was a miracle worker, during his life, and even after his death? In short, the answer to those two questions is what we will seek to find in this book. We desire the truth about this man's life, and about the events of October and November of 1929 when heaven seemed to touch earth.

The approach will be one of fairness, balance, accuracy, and objectivity. When dealing with the area of the unknown, in fact when dealing with anything that gets dubbed with the catch-all label "paranormal," it is best to simply lay out the facts as straightforward as possible, and then let the reader delve into that messy area of "belief." The method here is that of the historian and the journalist, not the missionary. In fact, mainstream historians have spent far too much time shying away from religion, and the supernatural, topics well suited and crying out for sober, fact-based, judgment-free prose. That is the goal for each chapter of this book.

Chapter one, "Life of Power," examines the mysterious life of this Irish born priest who never made it past the age of 25. It details such factors as Power's bloodline, and a curious similarity between this young man and other holy men and women throughout the history of the Catholic Church. These and other pieces of historical evidence serve to build a case for him as a potential miracle worker during his lifetime, and therefore perhaps after his death.

Chapter two, "29 Days in Autumn," chronicles the actual events of late October and November, 1929, when nearly a million pilgrims, literally from around the world, swarmed the grave of Father Power to seek his divine intercession. We will also look at the months and years leading up to this brief moment in history and see how Power's grave may have been a "wonder shrine" long before people were waiting in line for hours just to glimpse it.

Using previously unpublished materials, chapter three, "Closing the Gates," explains how and why the Archdiocese of Boston sealed Holy Cross, and how and why the diocese chose to move the body of Patrick Power to a new gravesite within the cemetery. This part of the book also looks at some of the letters that poured into the Boston chancery from people writing from across the globe, seeking help from the diocese, and ultimately from Father Power himself.

Also drawing on previously unpublished archival material, chapter four, "The Official Miracles," examines what appears to be the final report of the investigation conducted by the Archdiocese of Boston into the miracles said to have taken place at Power's grave in 1929. Just days after the gates of the cemetery closed, parish priests throughout the diocese began an inquiry into the alleged miracles said to have taken place among their parishioners who had visited the burial site. What they found is the subject of chapter four.

Finally, chapter five, "Letters of the Impossible," delves into the correspondence sent to the Boston chancery from people who claimed to have been miraculously healed by Patrick Power. Once again, this section draws from largely unpublished archival information, material not included in the chancery's official account.

Also a word on privacy. The Archdiocese of Boston was very gracious in granting permission to use archival material for this book. In return I have assured them that I will not use the names of any people who claimed to be miraculously healed by Father Power. This is meant to protect their privacy and the privacy of their families. The exception to this rule is if the name of the person in question was already published in local newspapers, something which can be checked in the endnotes, and in the appendix which has been assembled from media reports.

I again thank the archival department of the Archdiocese of Boston, particularly Archivist Robert Johnson Lally, for assistance in providing research materials and photographs. I also thank the Catholic Cemetery Association of the Archdiocese of Boston, located at Holy Cross Cemetery in Malden, Massachusetts, particularly Allen Burgess, and Richard Bradley. I would also like to extend a sincere thank you to my wife, Tammy, who took some of the photographs for this book and provided constant insight and support during its creation. Also, please keep in mind that this is the first book on Father Patrick Power, and by extension the first book on the events in Malden in late 1929. To say the least then, the existing published scholarship to draw from for this topic is therefore, shall we say, limited. In other words, if the Archdiocese of Boston and the Catholic Cemetery Association were not so forthcoming in opening their archives, what you are holding in your hands would simply not exist. The help and patience that they provided has been their miracle to me.

- John Koerner

Chapter One: Life of Power

Patrick Joseph Power entered and exited this world on exactly the same day, December 8, precisely 25 years apart. Although his life spanned only a quarter century, from 1844 to 1869, what happened in between those precious few years, and at his gravesite some 60 years later, still remain shrouded in speculation and mystery. Was this man a miracle worker, during his life, and even after his death? If so, why him? Furthermore, are there any clues in the scant biographical information that we have available to indicate that there was something divinely unique about this Irish priest? Certainly those who knew the man during his life seemed to think so, an opinion that lasted long after Power finished his earthly ministry.

Our quest to answer these questions though goes much further back, all the way to his ancestral background in Europe which is chock full of connections to religion, and even the paranormal. The Power,

1

Poher, or Poer family lineage in Ireland, of which Patrick Power can claim descent, at one time ranked among the most distinguished and notable in that country's history. The wealthy Simon de Poher contributed land and money to the abbey of the Blessed Virgin Mary in Dublin in 1187. In 1320, Milo Power began a twenty year stint as a bishop at Waterford County, the same location where an Edward Power soon after served as the last Abbot at the prestigious Mothel Monastery. From 1331 to 1339 alone, the family was said to claim at least nine barons and knights, one of whom was the celebrated Sir Roger de Poer, a successful Norman knight and warrior. A headland on the coast near County Cork even bears the name Power Head.[1]

Yet religion and chivalry were apparently not the only influences in Patrick Power's blood. Yes, even the subject of miracles creeps up in the Power family line. The Boston priest is almost certainly related to another reputed miracle worker in Ireland, a certain Father John Power whose shrine has also become a destination for pilgrims seeking the miraculous. According to Irish folklore, Father John first demonstrated his alleged power by curing an insane woman with water from a natural spring near his church. After Power's death, people began flocking to his grave to seek his divine help. They would often take with them samples of the earth that covered Father John's remains. Pilgrims would also leave crutches, braces, or other artifacts at the shrine, and at the local church in Rosecarbery where the late prelate had served.[2]

There are at least three factors that point to the strong likelihood that this Father Power was indeed related to Boston's Father Patrick Power. First, the surname is the same, not spelled Poer, or Poher, or some other variation which muddies the genealogical waters. Second, John was the name of Patrick Power's older brother, meaning that the name John made its way throughout this specific family tree. Finally, and most convincingly, Father John Power and Father Patrick Power both hailed from the same part of Ireland, County Cork. Not only that, both were from the town of Bantry in that part of the county. Unfortunately we do not know the exact time frame in which John Power lived except to say that he probably hailed from the eighteenth century. Nevertheless, the connection seems strong enough to provide some interesting speculation about Patrick Power's potentially miraculous genes, an ancestral inheritance that he might have carried throughout his lifetime.

This connection to Father John Power is only the first of many links to the miraculous that will surface time and again in Patrick's own life, long before the events of 1929 dubbed him as a wonder worker. Even the day that his mother gave birth to him, December 8, is now a day that Catholics use to celebrate one of the sacred unexplained mysteries of their religion. Since 1854, exactly 10 years after Father Power's birth in 1844, the eighth day of December has been known to the Catholic world as the Feast of the Immaculate Conception through a declaration given by Pope Pius IX. This dogma proclaims "that from the first moment of her conception, Mary – by the singular grace of God and by virtue of the merits of Jesus Christ – was preserved immune from original sin."[3] As we noted, Father Power also died on this same "stainless day" a quarter of a century later.[4]

By all accounts, this young man's brief life was not an easy one, filled with hard work, tragedy, and frequent illness. By the age of four, both of his parents, Patrick and Mary, were dead and he was forced to leave the little town of Bantry in County Cork, Ireland, where he and his three brothers and two sisters were born.[5] He left with his older brother John who decided to settle in with the bustling Irish community in Massachusetts, living variously in Cambridge, Fairmont, and Brookline. Very little is known about the early years of this newly arrived Irish child, except that he attended the Brookline elementary and preparatory schools, and later became an altar boy at the Church of the Most Holy Redeemer in East Boston. It was at this church that he met a man who would change his life.

Pastor James Fitton, founder of Holy Cross College in Worcester, took an immediate interest in the boy, sensing something exceptional about this urgent, quick to learn young man. Fitton taught him the Latin responses to the mass, grooming him for the priesthood, a desire that Power expressed early on.[6] It is likely that in Power's formative years, Fitton filled the void of the boy's two missing parents, a void that seemed to be increasingly satiated not just by this dedicated priest, but by in interest in the Catholic religion as well.

By the age of 17, Fitton decided that it was time for Patrick Power to begin his academic preparation for the priesthood. But where to send him? The pastor settled on Laval University in Quebec, Canada, for his altar boy to begin his studies, probably for three reasons. First, by the time Power reached the age of 17, it was now 1861 and the Civil War was brewing in the United States. Fitton likely wanted his young apprentice to be able to concentrate on his classes without the distraction of the war.

Second, had this young man remained in the United States a draft likely would have required him to serve in the military, and therefore postpone (or permanently end) his studies. In fact, these first two assumptions are backed up by an old record in the Laval University Library which describes Power as "an American come here because of the War of Secession."[7] To be sure though, this Irish lad was nothing if not patriotic for his new country, especially since he was well aware that the hated English were sympathetic towards the Confederacy. In the end, he never joined the military but suffered occasional jostling from his classmates who liked to point out to him American military failures in Quebec.[8]

The third reason Fitton selected Laval was that it was one of the best, not to mention one of the closest, seminaries in the Northeast making it a natural fit. Fitton practically paid for all of Power's theological education. For the first year alone the total fee for room, board, and tuition was $60. The Most Holy Redeemer pastor footed $40 of that bill, and the seminary remitted the balance of $20 through a scholarship that the young Irishman had obtained.[9] Unfortunately, neither Laval nor Fitton would see the fruits of their investments last the decade.

On September 4, 1861,[10] Power enrolled in the Petit, or Little, Seminary at Laval, a university that actually traces its roots back to 1663 when Msgr. Francis de Laval, the first bishop of New France, founded the Quebec Seminary with the direct authorization of King Louis XIV of France. A Royal Charter creating Laval University was granted to the Quebec Seminary by Queen Victoria in 1852. Laval still operates to this day boasting an enrollment of over 36,000 students with over 360 different degree programs. Laval stands as the first institution in North America to offer higher education in French,[11] a language that Power became quite fluent in.

This old institution of higher learning was nothing if not rigid. Students woke up at 5 a.m. during the fall and spring months of the school year. In the wintertime however the administration veritably allowed their pupils to slack off. They rose them at 5:30. This was followed closely on its heels by a 6 a.m. mass and a 7 a.m. breakfast. A few minutes of recreation were then permitted until the day's first lecture began which lasted until 10 a.m. Constant study, a break for lunch, and more classes consumed the rest of the day until 6 p.m. Students then had some free time until devotions at 6:30 p.m., followed immediately by supper, study, and then perhaps some socializing until evening prayers, just before the 9 p.m. curfew.[12] These young men would then get up and do this all over again the next day.

By all accounts, Power excelled at his studies. A record from February 1862 (five months into his academic career at Laval) stated the following: "Absences – none; conduct – excellent; work – excellent; memory – good and well trained."[13] A schoolmate of Power's during his two year stint in Canada was John O'Farrell who later became a priest at St. Louis De Gonsague Church in Quebec. O'Farrell's account of his memory of Patrick Power's days at Laval is one of the only surviving testimonies of any individual who had firsthand knowledge of Power.

I was only 13 years old when I entered the Petit Seminary on the same day that Power did, but he was a few years older and was placed in the division for the older boys while I remained in the class for the younger ones...

Power as I remember him, was a fine looking young man of medium height for his age, with an erect posture, but a rather frail build, except for his broad shoulders. His complexion was rather dark, his hair jet black and wavy, and he had striking, deep set, brown eyes.

Cleanliness of heart and mind from all evil was reflected in his countenance and when it was lighted up with a benign smile in greeting you, or flushed with religious fervor as he came from the altar, after receiving communion. It reminded you of holy and saintly pictures painted by the old masters.

His piety was evident to all who watched his conduct at
religious exercises and it was not put on for the occasion,
though it did not prevent him from indulging in wholesome,
boisterous sport during recreation periods, or taking part in an
occasional boyish prank.[14]

O'Farrell remembered one incident when Power was engaged in a race with another student in the halls of the seminary when all of a sudden two unsuspecting professors stepped out of an intersecting corridor and into their path. All four were sent sprawling.[15]

When not running down hallways and crashing into teachers, Power was busily earning the reputation as of one of the best scholars in the school, particularly in his mastery of French and Latin. In fact, it was probably during this time that he began to handwrite two books, likely finishing each between 1863 and 1864. The source materials for these works were no doubt the lectures that he attended at Laval, coupled with his own research, reading, and analysis. Each oversized volume was well over a foot in length, leather bound by Power himself, illustrated with his own pen drawings, and interwoven with various dried wild flowers, cloves, and maple leaves. Power signed at least one volume and listed his date of birth as December 8, 1844, giving us some solid evidence that he was indeed born on the Immaculate Conception, as was mentioned earlier. The books delved into such areas as astronomy, natural philosophy, chemistry, mathematics, botany, physics, and theology; one written in French, the other in Latin. These gems were handed down through the Power family, and by the time of the 1929 Malden miracles had made their way into the hands of Edmund J. Power, of Boston, a nephew of Father Power.[16]

Besides the scientific topics that this young seminarian felt compelled to inscribe for posterity, he also included a thesis on the possibility of miracles. Yes, that's right, miracles. This is now the second time in his biography that this idea of the miraculous has cropped up with him, and as we will see it will not be the last. First, we detailed how the supernatural may be a part of the Power bloodline. Now Power himself tells us by writing this thesis that the subject weighed on his own mind. Why? I think it is reasonable to ask that if miracles were attributed to this man after he died, was he also a miracle worker in his own lifetime? Although we do not have a definite answer to this question, we do have some clues, some hints that Patrick Power may have indeed been a wonder worker during his brief time on this earth. The fact that he wrote a detailed analysis of miracles, and in the process seemed intimately acquainted with the topic, as if reciting a secret family recipe, makes us conclude that he must have had some firsthand knowledge and experience with this subject matter. Consider that what you are about to read was written by an individual who had not yet reached the age of twenty, but who wrote like an aged theologian. Although the essay was no doubt on some level informed by his schoolwork, nevertheless this is what Patrick Power had to say about the miraculous.

A miracle is a sensible work performed by God and surpassing the order of all created sensible nature. The purpose of a miracle is to manifest something to man. Such a way is that which appeals to the senses.

To be a true miracle there should be either no creative forces in the sensible world capable of effecting it, or if there are any such forces they should not be used here and now to bring about the event that is called miraculous.

The purpose of a miracle is the moral good of man, especially his supernatural good. Thus God performs a miracle either to show his goodness toward some individual or to make manifest the sanctity of one of His saints or to prove the divine mission of one of His messengers. Briefly, the purpose of a miracle is some good in the moral order.

Such works are possible because the forces of nature are finite, and hence their effects have only a limited amount of perfection. But God is infinite. Hence it is possible to have effects which far exceed in perfection those found in nature. These works are possible because God is omnipotent.

Such works are possible because God, who is omnipotent, can do alone and immediately that which He ordinarily does by means of secondary causes in a slow and gradual manner. For example, He can create immediately new cells in a decayed arm.

When a miracle is performed, the physical law is only suspended. It does not produce its effect. But the law itself is not necessarily changed. Moreover, when God decreed the law he also decreed the exceptions He would make to the law.

In order that a miracle be known with certainty, a three-fold truth should be known. That is, the historical truth of the miracle – whether the event said to be miraculous really took place. Second, the philosophical truth of the miracle; that is whether this work or fact was above the order of all created sensible nature.

Was there no occult law or force of nature that could bring about this event? We here suppose the historical truth to have been proven, and we seek the further truth as to whether it transcended the force of nature. Third, the theological truth of the miracle. That is, whether this sensible work which as we suppose has been proved to be an historical fact and to have surpassed the order of all created sensible nature, was really done by God or that some creature at the command of God is at least the moral cause of it.[17]

Essentially, Patrick Power believed that true miracles came from God, transcended science, and were proved beyond historical doubt to have actually taken place. This logical three-fold formula however is not what stands out the most in this thesis. One line veritably jumps off the page. Power says, "For example, He can create immediately new cells in a decayed arm." Why include an example of a miracle? Moreover, why include *this* example? There are no other illustrative points made in the thesis, no explanatory examples made in his three-fold formula, nor in his initial theological argumentation. Therefore the inclusion of an example at any point in the analysis seems odd. Also, consider the illustration that he chose. He did not choose a classic, "generic" miracle such as healing the blind, or curing the diseased. Instead, his example is curiously specific and obscure. It seems logical then to at least suggest that Power may have had firsthand knowledge of the healing of a "decayed arm," knowledge perhaps obtained through his own hands. Let us then consider the odd inclusion of this almost offhanded remark as "exhibit c" in our case to build Patrick Power as a miracle worker.

The trail does not run cold there however. We may even be able to trace Patrick Power's interest in miracles, and in turn perhaps his ability to perform them, to a specific location. As a seminarian, this young man made repeated pilgrimages to the nearby shrine of Saint Anne de Beaupre, long reputed to be a miraculous shrine. This basilica dedicated to St. Anne, the mother the Blessed Virgin Mary, is located in the village of Beaupre, approximately 25 miles northeast of Quebec City. In the 1650s, several shipwrecked sailors in the Gulf of St. Lawrence believed that they had been saved by the intercession of St. Anne. In thanksgiving they decided to build a chapel in her honor at the nearby village of Beaupre.[18] During construction of the church in 1658, the healing of a man by the name of Louis Guimond allegedly took place, said to be the first of countless other miracles that would follow. A larger stone and wood church was built in 1661 to accommodate an ever greater number of the faithful seeking the miraculous, followed by an even grander construction in 1676 which stood for exactly two centuries. This was the church that Patrick Power paid his visits to as a young man. 1876 saw the opening of the Basilica of St. Anne, far more magnificent than its three predecessors. It stood until March 29, 1922, when a fire brought it to the ground. Its replacement, which still stands today, was constructed the following year and can easily accommodate more than 3,000 people on any given day.[19]

Yet through all of its various incarnations, one element has remained constant, the healings. Through the centuries people have left crutches, canes, wheelchairs, and other artifacts at the shrine as evidence of their belief that St. Anne has interceded on their behalf. The healing power of the basilica is said to flow from the fountain in front of the church. 1.5 million visitors make the journey to this shrine each year.[20] In 1861, 1862, and 1863 one among them was Patrick Power. A telling story survives from one of the times that Power visited the shrine during these years. Apparently one day he noticed an usually large number of deformed and crippled children praying inside the church, a sight which brought him to tears. Power is said to have remarked "How I wish I might be able to do something to relieve the sufferings of these little ones." A fellow seminarian who made the journey with him replied "Well, now you are Power by name, but some day you may have the power to cure."[21]

It seems likely that these pilgrimages to the shrine were transformative experiences for this young man. Certainly if nothing else he could see that miracles were not just something to read about in theological treatises, but instead were real life events happening to actual people asking for divine intercession. Keep in mind that it is not uncommon for a reputed miracle worker to draw strength and inspiration from a known miraculous site. Father Nelson Baker, of Buffalo, a documented practitioner of the supernatural from the same generation as Patrick Power, also had a transformative pilgrimage to a known miraculous shrine. Like Power, this journey took place while Baker was a seminarian. The Buffalo man took a trip to Europe in 1874 and twice visited the Our Lady of Victory Basilica in Paris, France. There he viewed canes, crutches, wheelchairs, iron braces, and other artifacts left by people who claimed to be healed through the intercession of the Blessed Virgin Mother.[22] This was the moment in the life of Nelson Baker when he decided to dedicate his life to Mary in her title as Our Lady of Victory, later constructing a magnificent basilica to honor her name. This was also arguably the turning point in Baker's miraculous life as well, a time when he resolved to strive to heal people through the intercession of Our Lady of Victory, incidentally the only source he cited when people dubbed him a wonder worker.

Could it have been the same for Patrick Power? Unfortunately, history has not recorded if Power carried a devotion to St. Anne throughout the rest of his short ministry. However, his persistent interest in a known "miracle shrine" and his altruistic, expressed desire to heal other human beings certainly raise some eyebrows and add to the portfolio we are building for him as a wonder worker. At minimum we can conclude that the subject of the miraculous probably entered the life of Patrick Power during his time at Laval Seminary, evidenced in his thesis on miracles and in his journeys to Beaupre.

From left to right, three priests from the Church of the Most Holy Redeemer in East Boston, Father Casson, Father Fitton, and Father Power. Father Fitton would be Patrick Power's lifelong mentor. Power is 23 years-old in this photograph.

International Newsreel courtesy of Archdiocese of Boston Archives

Power stayed at Laval until 1863 when he was nineteen years old.[23]
However, he was not ordained until 1867, some four years later. Little
is known about these intervening years except that after his stint in
Canada he attended at least one or perhaps two more seminaries to
complete his coursework for the priesthood. The one institution that
Power definitely attended after leaving Laval was the University of
Louvain in Belgium where he exclusively studied theology.[24] The other
school in question was St. Joseph's Seminary in Troy, New York. In all
likelihood he went directly to Belgium after finishing at Laval since the
Civil War was still raging in 1863. Logically then, Power would not return to the United States until after the war ended in April 1865. This
would give him enough time to enroll for the fall semester in 1865 at
St. Joseph's, perhaps staying for two years of course work, ending in the
spring of 1867 just a few months before he was ordained.

This chronology fits, but it is hard to substantiate the second half
of it. The idea that Power went to St. Joseph's comes from limited biographical media reports which surrounded the Malden miracles of
1929.[25] One report in question was even accompanied by inaccuracies,
such as placing Power's ordination in Troy, which as we will see below
is patently false. No reports even guess at the dates that the Boston
seminarian attended the Troy seminary. Unfortunately the trail runs
cold there. St. Joseph's Seminary closed its doors for good in 1957.[26] A
check of the Troy Historical Society and the Albany Diocesan Archives

yielded nothing in the way of student records from the seminary, much less anything about Patrick Power.

So we are left with guesswork, frustratingly losing four years of this man's life into an abyss, years that may have seen him mature as a practitioner of the miraculous. We do know however that he was ordained on September 7, 1867, at the Cathedral of the Holy Cross in Boston by Bishop J. J. Williams of the Boston Diocese.[27] An original ordination card for the event reads "In Memory of Sept. 7th, 1867, (Eve of the Feast of the Nativity) of the B.V.M. (Blessed Virgin Mary) whereon Rev. Patrick J. Power Received the Holy Orders of Priesthood in the Cathedral Chapel of the Holy Cross Boston, Mass."[28] After being ordained, Power had only 822 days to live. He seems to have divided his time between at least three parishes, the Church of the Most Holy Redeemer in East Boston, St. Matthew's Church in Chicopee, and St. Michael's Church in Springfield.

There are two pieces of evidence to connect him to Most Holy Redeemer. First, while dressed in his priestly vestments Power posed for a formal portrait with Fr. Fitton, pastor of Most Holy Redeemer Parish.[29] The fact that Power donned his sacred garments for this photograph indicates that the picture must date from a point in time after his ordination. Fitton was of course his life long mentor so it seems likely that Power would have been a frequent, perhaps even unofficial, prelate of this parish. The second piece of evidence to support his presence at Most Holy Redeemer is the fact that the children of that parish raised the money to pay for the tombstone which still rests over Power's remains at Holy Cross Cemetery.[30] This logically then would indicate that Power must have spent a great deal of his time ministering to these little ones and getting to know the parish children personally for them to make such a gesture.

Power's time at St. Matthew's, and at St. Michael's, were apparently more of the official variety. In July 1869, the young priest was assigned by the bishop to be an assistant to the Rev. Patrick Healy in Springfield, Massachusetts, after the death of Pastor M. P. Gallagher in June of that year at St. Michael's. Yet Power also split his precious remaining time with at least one other church in the immediate area, that being St. Matthew's in Chicopee.[31] Power's service in the Springfield area can thus be narrowed down to just a few months before his death. Since there were no other churches associated with his tenure as a priest, he must have spent his initial ministry in East Boston at Most Holy Redeemer before being reassigned to Springfield where we know he became quite ill just days before meeting his death, as we will see below.

Yet it is from his brief stint in Springfield that we have a rare archival gem from a woman with firsthand knowledge of Power. On December 29, 1929, the Archdiocese of Boston received a letter from Ellen Morrissey of Indian Orchard, Massachusetts. Morrissey's letter detailed an interview that she conducted with her mother who knew the young priest personally. According to the detailed missive, Power came to Indian Orchard, near Springfield, to hear confessions, and would then stay overnight at the house of Ellen Morrissey's mother, which was next to the church. Apparently Power was sent there because of a heavy French population in the area.

> Father Power came frequently because of his ability to preach in the French language…(H)e would preach two sermons each Sunday, one in English, and one in French…Father Power was able to bring about greater harmony between the people of the two nationalities.
>
> He had a very pleasing voice and he sang the mass beautifully. He was very fond of children and they would flock around him when he appeared. He had a refined, sensitive nature, and a very pleasant manner…
>
> He went back to Ireland during the time that he was studying in Europe. He remembered the place very clearly and could find a little gap in a hedge through which he had climbed when he was a child.[32]

Morrissey's mother also remembered a Saturday night when Power was very ill. "He coughed incessantly during the night," she recounted. A mustard plaster was applied "but he spent a very bad night…From the symptoms they felt that he had tuberculosis at that time." Ellen Morrissey stated that her mother "had no difficulty in recalling these memories because they have been kept fresh in her memory through repetition."[33]

As we noted above, Power's time in Springfield was at the end of his ministry. Therefore, the young prelate's disease-ridden, restless Saturday night, recounted above, may in fact have taken place just a few days before he died. When his superior, Fr. Healy, realized how sick Power had become, he sent for Patrick's brother John in Brookline. The elder Power came immediately and brought his younger brother to his home on Fairmont Street in Brookline.[34] It was there that Father Patrick Joseph Power died on December 8, 1869. At his bedside was his ten year old nephew, Edmund J. Power, son of his brother, John. "He passed away about 4 o'clock in the afternoon," Edmund recounted in 1929. "It was unexpected; there was just mother and father and I and the doctor at the bedside. He was conscious to the end, and quiet, murmuring prayer."[35] Power likely died of either double lobar pneumonia, or tuberculosis, two very similar ailments.[36]

The funeral for this young priest was far from the ordinary, filled with several unusual moments and details. The body of Father Power stayed at the home of his brother until December 10 when a hearse and a team of horses arrived to transport the late prelate. According to E. J. Power, Patrick Power's nephew, as soon as the horses reached the Brookline house, a strange change came over them. The team instantly bolted down the hill at breakneck speed, overturned the hearse, and nearly killed the driver who skillfully managed to save his own life. Coming up the same hill, John Power looked upon the scene horrified, thinking the casket had already been put in the hearse. To his relief, it was still safely inside the house.[37] Is it strange that these animals seemed unwilling to send Power's body to its final resting place?

Despite a driving snowstorm, the funeral party eventually made it safely to the Church of the Most Holy Redeemer in East Boston where Father Fitton said the mass of requiem. Priests are invariably buried in purple robes, a symbol of sorrow. Pastor Fitton, the closest thing Patrick Power had to a father, had his young apprentice dressed and buried in white vestments, a symbol of purity, innocence, and glory.[38] At one point the services were interrupted because Fitton was unable to control what must have been an overwhelming sense of sorrow and loss. He openly broke down in front of the congregation and began to audibly weep,[39] obviously a display of emotion rarely seen in the head officiate at a funeral mass.

Power was buried that same day, December 10, the first priest to be interred at the recently opened Holy Cross Cemetery in Malden.[40] He was laid to rest with a white floral wreath, made by his brother John, and a golden chalice that he used in Mass during his priesthood.[41] According to local folklore, the golden chalice that rested in the hands of the deceased Patrick Power was the model for the chalice carved into the marble headstone which rests above his remains at Holy Cross Cemetery.[42] This very carving in the slab collected rainwater and would be at the center of some of the miraculous claims made many years later as we will see in the next chapter.

Another revealing aspect to the Power funeral services was the eulogy, presumably given by Fitton at the gravesite. It is a touching, personal, poetic effort filled with soaring religious imagery, and hinting at intriguing biographical details.

Death's angels pale another sainted soul,
Has rescued from the stormy sea of life
To treasures in an Eden where no care
Or tribulations for the goods of earth
Can find an entrance in the bloom of youth.
With golden honors clustering around
His brow and giving expectations bright
Of guerdons redolent of priestly worth.
Our friend has passed away manly and true.
Of sympathetic nature, pure, refined,
Childlike and gentle in his every act.
His very smile gained friends and tried as gold
In crucible of alchemist. His worth
Shines brighter from the silent pangs endured
In his long lingering disease which cast
Its baleful shade over him. Hopeful still.
Pure in his conscience, to no man a foe,
He calmly passed from earth while Mary's fame
In vast cathedral pile and cloistered wall
Was sweet recited by her children dear,
And caught in strains of melody sublime,
By seraph hosts and cherubim above.
Beneath the snow dear Father Power now rests in placid calm.
No more his voice be heard in converse sweet;
No more in sanctuary will silver notes
Swell through the fretted aisles in God's great praise.
For stilled forever in this fading earth
Must rest that tongue all eloquent in song.
Peace to his ashes! Grant him glory, love,
In thy own martyr band enroll our dead.

Mary, fair patroness, thy child receive
As on the day he died, angelic chimes
Another soul is added to your host...[43]

There are two aspects to the eulogy that stand out. First, Fitton characterized Power as "sainted," a word not lightly applied by a trained and educated religious man who knew exactly what the literal and figurative connotations of such a word entailed. Second, the eulogy tells us "His worth shines brighter from the silent pangs endured in his long lingering disease which cast its baleful shade over him." Stated plainly, Father Power did not enjoy good health. Such a conclusion seems strengthened by the fact that this man's body could not take him past the age of 25. We may reasonably conclude from this that Patrick Power lived a life of physical suffering which eventually wore him down to an early death. His very eulogy supports this. Why is this important? Above all else it intrigues us because intense holiness mixed with personal physical suffering has long been a recipe for the miraculous. Therefore we can add "the silent pangs endured" by Patrick Power as yet another factor in our case to build Power as a practitioner of the supernatural.

We look to history for precedent. One parallel with Power lies in a man from his own generation, Father Nelson Baker, of Buffalo (1841/1842-1936). Baker, now on the path to sainthood, was also a man of intense holiness who endured a great deal of physical suffering in his own life as well. The Buffalo prelate remarkably recovered from a near fatal skin disease during his days at Niagara Falls Suspension Bridge Seminary, and later in his life had one of his eyes removed in the mid-1920s. Perhaps not coincidentally, during Baker's life, and even after his death, scores of people attributed skin-related, or eye-related miracles to his intercession.[44]

Other examples of suffering linked with the miraculous come from many classic saints of the Catholic Church. Sebastian, a fourth century saint, allegedly miraculously recovered from a slew of arrows meant to execute him. His convalescence led many to believe that he had an inexplicable immunity to epidemics and diseases and later was credited with interceding on the behalf of many European cities suffering under raging illnesses, such as Lisbon and Milan in the 1500s.[45]

A woman born in the same year as Patrick Power, St. Bernadette of Lourdes (1844-1879), lived a similar life to the Boston priest in at least one respect. She died young, at the age of 35, and lived a life of constant weakness and illness, including bouts with debilitating asthma. Nevertheless, the Catholic Church has recognized 65 miracles attributed to the intercession of Bernadette, born Marie Bernard Soubirous. Beginning at the age of 14, she claimed to have visions of the Blessed Virgin Mary in the town of Lourdes, France. During one of these visions a spring began to flow out of the mouth of a cave. To this day people insist that the water still has the same curative properties that people claimed it apparently did in the 1800s.[46]

We might also mention the renowned Italian priest and mystic Padre Pio (1887-1968), canonized in 2002. Pio endured 50 years of bleeding and intense pain as a result of receiving the five wounds of the crucified Christ (feet, hands, and abdomen) known as the stigmata. Countless miracles have been attributed to Pio, including the phenomenon of bilocation (appearing in two places simultaneously). The miracle used to canonize the late prelate involved the case of a boy who had advanced meningitis and suddenly recovered after Padre Pio's apparent intercession.[47]

Why the correlation between suffering and miracles? To answer this question we must pose a larger one. How does a human being attain supernatural power? Certainly intense holiness seems to be a part of the answer, but it still leaves us guessing because countless individuals throughout history have been intensely holy and yet unable to perform miracles. Think of your local parish priest, or minister, for example. Therefore there must be another piece to the puzzle. There must be another level of understanding. In looking at the evidence, I think in the cases of many holy and sainted men and women throughout history, that other piece of the puzzle is often the endurance of intense personal, physical suffering. When dealing with the realm of the miraculous, with the idea of healing and helping others, perhaps one must first know what it means to suffer, (and then sometimes be healed) in order to know what it means to heal another human being. Perhaps miracles have everything to do with a profoundly mysterious, physical, and then spiritual, empathy.

Certainly in the case of Patrick Power intense holiness and suffering played key roles in his life. Having now looked at what we know of this life, we pose the question again. Was Patrick Power a miracle worker during his lifetime? The pieces are certainly there for him. We can point to his potentially miraculous bloodline, his birth and death on the Immaculate Conception, his visits to the shrine of St. Anne de Beaupre, his thesis on miracles, the example he used within that thesis, and finally the mix of suffering and holiness that typified his life. In the final analysis this may be the closest that we will ever get to answering this question because of one simple, frustrating fact. "I don't think it was documented," said Richard Bradley, director of Operations for the Catholic Cemetery Association of the Archdiocese of Boston at Holy Cross Cemetery in Malden. "A lot of people didn't read and write then. There were a lot of immigrants."

Nevertheless, Bradley insists that there was something special about this priest. "I don't think he was just an ordinary guy. He had to be far from ordinary to have accomplished all that he did in such a short time. I think he was anything but ordinary."[48] However, Power's apparent extraordinary nature is ironically perhaps more easily demonstrated not by his life, but by events which happened many years after his death. As it turned out, December 8, 1869, would not be the last time that the world would hear from Patrick Power.

Chapter Two: 29 Days in Autumn

Firemen from nearby Charlestown, MA, pray on November 15, 1929, for the recovery of a firefighter who had been paralyzed for 12 years.

International Newsreel courtesy of Archdiocese of Boston Archives

Holy Cross Cemetery in Malden is at 175 Broadway. This is a simple but perhaps not insignificant fact in our investigation into the miraculous. For many centuries Malden's Broadway was an ancient Native American road which led to the Newbury area. This well worn path was then a natural choice to use as a major road for the colonists who began settling in Malden, probably around the year 1632.[49]

Why is the history of Broadway as a Native American causeway significant? To answer this question we need to briefly enter the world of dowsable energy lines and ley lines. Dowsable energy lines are lines of energy whose direction and existence can be found by a complex scientific process known as dowsing. Such lines can be below the ground or above the ground.[50] Ley lines are thought to have been marked and surveyed by ancient peoples including Native Americans. It is speculated that these lines were marked and surveyed in an effort to align certain geographical sites. It is possible that all ley lines connecting sites are dowsable energy lines.[51]

Native American roads are often thought by researchers to be prime candidates for dowsable energy lines, flowing with active geological energy. Some of the latest research in this field suggests that Native Americans may have deliberately built sacred sites along these energy lines. The point of all this speculation is to suggest that perhaps Holy Cross Cemetery may sit on a dowsable energy line, recognized as such by Native Americans, centuries beforehand. Does Broadway have sacred, dowsable, geological energy flowing through it? The point here is not to answer that question, but simply to raise it in speculation and add it to the mystery of the cemetery. In short, does Holy Cross Cemetery possess some sort of earth energy?

Holy Cross was consecrated on September 27, 1868, as a much-needed burial ground for the people of Malden, Brighton, Roxbury, Belmont, and other surrounding suburbs. It was purchased by a Somerville funeral home director named Patrick Rafferty, incidentally the same funeral director who buried Father Power. Today there are close to 400,000 bodies buried in Holy Cross and another 3,000 in the recently constructed mausoleum.[52] It is a massive field of the dead.

Deep in the folklore of the cemetery is the idea that for decades the grave of Patrick Power was a sacred site, long before the events of 1929 made it famous. The *Boston Daily Globe* noted this on November 13, 1929.

> Although the grave of Rev. Fr. Patrick J. Power has only recently become the scene of pilgrimages on a large scale, it has for more than 30 years been an object of veneration on the part of Malden and Everett folk.
>
> An Everett resident recalls that when he was a boy, 30 years ago, his mother used to take him to Fr. Power's grave for a brief prayer for the dead priest. Apparently Fr. Power's memory was revered for some special reason at that time.
>
> There is also talk among the older residents of these two cities (Everett and Malden) of a reported cure that took place at the grave about 30 years ago.[53]

If the Everett boy mentioned above was praying at the grave in 1899 with his mother, the idea that it was a special burial site must have even pre-dated this date, otherwise why would the family single out Power's grave? Therefore the Power legend must have already been in place for many years at that point.

There are other sources we can point to in building the case for pre-1929 Power miracles. Holy Cross Cemetery Assistant Superintendent Joseph Walsh submitted a report to the Boston Archdiocese chancery on December 1, 1929, which detailed the events of the previous month at Holy Cross. Like the *Globe* article, Walsh also noted that talk of miraculous cures related to Father Power pre-dated 1929.

> As nearly as I can remember, about three years ago (1926) my attention was first called to visitors at the monument on his grave. I noticed people dipping their fingers into the water in the depression where the chalice is cut and blessing themselves. I questioned one of them regarding their doing it and was informed (that)…special benefits were derived from the use of the water with prayer…At different times I had heard of cures which took place there. I am unable to state whether they were authentic or not…Many of the old gravediggers daily had the habit of going past that stone first thing in the morning and blessing themselves.[54]

Walsh also noted that at different times he would notice groups of people gathered at the grave to pray. Later in his letter, Walsh recounted the details of a specific miracle said to have taken place about 30 years prior. He received word of the story directly via two sisters from Chelsea, Massachusetts, who claimed that their brother "was threatened with blood poisoning in his leg." Walsh wrote that "the sisters took some of the rain water which had collected in the chalice and rubbed it on his leg. The next day he was completely cured. The sisters said nothing about the cure at the time and now they are telling everyone."[55]

F. Lauriston Bullard's 1930 article entitled "Malden – In Retrospect and Prospect" seems to corroborate this story from the two Chelsea women. Bullard stated that he collected information from a conversation that he had with an unnamed priest from the diocese. He placed the alleged healing in approximately 1897.

> A spike had been drive into a man's leg, a friend in wrenching
> it away tore the flesh, gangrene set in, and the wound appeared
> incurable. A sister anointed the limb with water from the
> chalice above the grave. There were several applications. Slowly,
> not instantaneously, the leg healed. Said the priest: "He told me
> it was like magic. That was his word – 'magic'"
>
> In the course of thirty years or more a few other cures
> were associated with the tomb. A deaf boy was made to
> hear. Reverent Catholics passing the cemetery would cross
> themselves with the name of Father Power upon their lips.[56]

Therefore in looking at the above evidence we are evidently dealing with four independent sources here. The first one is the *Globe* article, apparently based on interviews with Everett and Malden residents. The second source is Walsh's own firsthand memory and observations of behavior at the cemetery. The third source is the interview that Walsh conducted with the two Chelsea sisters, recounted in his report to the chancery. The final source is Bullard's article, which describes the same event as the one told to Walsh by the Chelsea sisters. However, we can consider it a separate source because the origin of the Bullard account is a local priest, not the sisters. All four sources leave us then with only one logical conclusion. The grave of Father Patrick Power was considered a "Miracle Shrine" long before the events of 1929.

One might reasonably ask, why were these people singling out Power's grave in the first place? In chapter one, we documented several pieces of evidence to suggest that Power may have been a miracle worker during his lifetime. We might now add another piece to the puzzle. The fact that people went to Power's grave decades before 1929 to seek his divine intervention suggests that Power likely had a reputation for the miraculous during his brief lifetime which carried over after his death. Why else would people seek out this specific gravesite? There were other priests buried in "The Clergymen's Lot" that people could have chosen over the years, including the much more famous Father Fitton who was buried right next to him. Instead, Patrick Power was singled out for decades by area residents, many of whom probably knew him firsthand.

So how then did the alleged miraculous ability of Patrick Power move from being a local legend to a national phenomenon? The answer to this question hinges on the events of a key date, October 27, 1929. On that day, Pastor Patrick H. Walsh of St. Joseph's Church in Malden decided to mention in his Sunday sermon that at various times he had heard reports about miracles connected with the grave of Father Patrick Power at nearby Holy Cross Cemetery.[57] Hearing this long rumored idea from an official source, the parishioners of St. Joseph's began circulating this information. This must have seemed to many as a validation of the fact that the Power grave was in fact a miracle shrine, something suspected long before 1929, as was demonstrated above.

Another key player in this unfolding drama was Mrs. Mary O'Hearn of Franklin Avenue in Everett, Massachusetts. Sometime between the end of Walsh's sermon on Sunday, October 27, and the date of Tuesday, October 29, this Everett woman made it known that after three visits to the Power burial site during the previous summer, her hearing was allegedly restored.[58] Tuesday, October 29, was the date that two inquisitive reporters showed up at the offices of Holy Cross Cemetery in Malden with the name of Mary O'Hearn on their lips. They were there to get the official version of events before proceeding. However, these two journalists came away with precious little.

"On Tuesday, October 29, this year, two men approached me in the office and one of them asked me what I knew about the cures at Father Power's grave. I told them I knew nothing whatsoever," wrote Assistant Superintendent Walsh in his December 1, 1929 letter to the

Archdiocese. "He then informed me that he was a reporter and that he had questioned a Mrs. Mary O'Hearn of Franklin Avenue, Everett, who claimed she had been cured of deafness which a specialist said was incurable."[59] Although Walsh apparently did not have any information regarding the O'Hearn case, nor for another case that the reporter mentioned, he did want to know if this newspaperman intended to publish what he had uncovered so far. According to Walsh, the reporter answered "'not at this time.' I asked him to hold off on any story regarding the same as the cemetery did not wish to have it published until it was more authentic. He promised he would not print the same until he received word from the cemetery."

This journalist would never receive any official word from the cemetery or the archdiocese, nor would anyone else for that matter regarding the "authenticity" of what had happened, or what was about to happen at Holy Cross Cemetery.[60] Therefore the decision the following day to print the O'Hearn information may have seemed at the time to be rash, but in retrospect, no archdiocesan sanction would have been handed down anyway. So on October 30, 1929, much to the consternation of Patrick Walsh, the *Malden Evening News* became the first newspaper to print word of the alleged cures at the Power gravesite.[61] Before long other newspapers picked up the baton. By Halloween, the *Boston Daily Globe* had the story on its front page, above the fold, with a photograph of the grave under the heading "Tomb Of Priest Becomes

Shrine For Afflicted Folk."[62] The *New York Times* joined in for the first time on November 11 with a front page article below the fold with the title "Miracle Seekers in Crush at Cemetery Shrine; Police Forced to Remove Priest's Gravestone."[63]

Onlookers at Holy Cross Cemetery watch a man attempt to walk unassisted on November 13, 1929.

International Newsreel courtesy of Archdiocese of Boston Archives

Meanwhile, Mary O'Hearn was telling anyone who would listen about what had happened to her earlier that year. "I became stone deaf after one of my children died last May," she told a reporter on Halloween, 1929. "[W]hile caring for him I contracted severe abscesses of the ear which finally destroyed my hearing. I was totally deaf and the physicians said the condition would be permanent." After hearing of the "cures" at the grave, O'Hearn decided to go to the cemetery to pray and anoint herself with rainwater from the stone chalice on the tombstone. "I went three times," she said. "Shortly after my third visit last August I woke up one morning and found that my hearing had been restored to me."[64]

Assistant Superintendent Walsh picks up the narrative from there. "On Thursday, October 31, about 300 came out to the grave and prayed. On Friday, November 1, about 1,000 were at the grave…On Sunday, November 3 over 10,000 persons visited the grave," he wrote in his official report to the diocese. "From November 5 to November 24 the crowd varied from 50,000 to 125,000 on the last day."[65] The newspapers placed the numbers higher. 200,000 were said to have visited on November 18 alone.[66] In all, estimates of total visitors to the Power grave that autumn ranged from 847,000, to a cool million.[67]

Whatever the numbers were, the goal of everyone was the same, to get to the gravesite. Eventually two lines to that coveted spot formed, one from the Lynn Street gates, and the other from the Broadway entrance. Occasionally these lines would be two abreast and even a third line was formed for invalids and cripples who could not stay in the regular lines.[68] This provided for a fairly efficient manner of getting to the grave as quickly as possible whereupon the pilgrims would be asked by cemetery workers and guards to linger only briefly before proceeding up the hill to All Souls' Chapel for a short prayer. Unfortunately though, despite this system of moving as many pilgrims to the site as possible, countless individuals on any given day missed the chance to reach the grave because of the crush of people. To ensure success, thousands resorted to camping overnight outside the gates to be the first ones inside once they were swung open again.[69]

With so many miracle seekers fixated on reaching the Power marker, it was not long before the grave itself quickly became littered with mementos of these quick visits. Flowers, coins, rosaries, medals, pictures, and statues, were left on the tombstone while even the chapel filled with crutches, braces, eyeglasses, and other signs of the crippled. In early December 1929, Walsh submitted an inventory to the chancery of these items left at the chapel and the burial site. These were the ones that he knew about. "We have in our possession the following articles left by different persons at the grave and chapel," he wrote on December 4. "1 cast, 9 canes, 12 crutches, 7 iron leg braces worn by children, 2 iron adult braces, 2 hand splints, 1 leather brace, 23 pair eyeglasses, 1 pair arch supports."[70]

As time went on, more and more people entered the cemetery office to tell Walsh all about their miraculous stories. On Friday, November 1, he got word that Margaret McManus had been cured of "ulcerous varicose veins which she had for many years."[71] On November 6 a woman from Lawrence, Massachusetts, "claimed that she was cured of failing eyesight. She left her glasses on the slab of the grave." That same day a woman from Malden also told Walsh that "she had been cured of serious eye trouble which almost made her blind." The following day a four year old child left her crutches at the grave. "Her mother said that her legs were paralyzed since birth. I personally saw this happen,"[72] Walsh noted.

Edward J. O'Connell, left, Superintendent of Holy Cross Cemetery, conferring with a policeman. O'Connell personally oversaw the security of Holy Cross Cemetery, and later the removal of Father Power's body.
International Newsreel courtesy of Archdiocese of Boston Archives

Apparently this was not the only miracle that the assistant super-intendent eyewitnessed. In his December 4 report to the diocese he related a remarkable story that he saw unfold in front of his eyes. At his side was a man named Michael Williams, editor of New York City's *Commonweal* magazine. Walsh saw a 14 year old boy from Readville, Massachusetts, kneel in front of the grave, jump up, hold his bended leg, and then burst into tears. "Between his sobs he informed me that he was able to bend his knee, something he could never do before. He said he couldn't help crying he was so happy. Mr. Williams stated that it was the most wonderful thing he had ever seen,"[73] Walsh said.

For his part, Williams also wrote about this remarkable event in his own magazine in December 1929. "The boy uttered a sharp cry and soon was moving his leg freely at the knee joint, which, his relatives said, had been immovable for years," Williams reported. "In the center of a small group of excited people, praying or exclaiming, the boy was taken away, walking, though slowly and painfully, to the chapel."[74]

During his time at the cemetery, Williams not only witnessed the above alleged miracle, but he also was able to secure what ended up being the closest thing to an official statement that any high ranking Catholic official would ever make regarding the events at Malden. The statement came from E. J. O'Connell, superintendent at Holy Cross Cemetery, and brother to Archbishop Cardinal William O'Connell. Since O'Connell's words remain the nearest guess we have at what the diocese was thinking at the time, it is worth quoting from it at some length. The statement to Williams is laced with bewilderment, frustration, and even some fear.

> We cannot possibly accept responsibility, or even appear to give anything resembling authoritative endorsement to what is going on. It is a situation for which we are not responsible... We have been very much alarmed, fearful of disorder, or that some serious accident or panic might develop. It has required all the resources of our local police force, assisted by volunteers from the fire department and sometimes by policemen from nearby communities, in addition to our own cemetery staff to handle the crowd.[75]

Williams then asked O'Connell what he thought about the reports of miracles. "I know no more than you do," he replied, "and am no more competent than you to render an opinion." Interestingly though, the superintendent could have stopped there, but he chose not to. What he said next hinted at privileged information.

> I only know that for years there has been a certain amount of talk, in restricted quarters, concerning Father Power's grave. As to the supposed cures, you can see for yourself the signed statements of several doctors which have been left at this office, in which they testify to the sudden and remarkable cures or improvement of their own patients. The newspapers have been full of other cases, some of them exceedingly striking, others of very slight consequences, most of them, of course, unverified. All that we know here at the cemetery is that we have been flooded by a tide of humanity...[76]

E. J. Connell's brother, the archbishop, had a similar opportunity to make a public statement about the Malden events. He visited the grave on November 12 and then again on November 16. On Tuesday, November 12, he arrived alone and unannounced, standing silently in observation next to the grave as the lines moved past him. Afterwards he spent a few minutes in prayer at All Souls' Chapel and emerged to face reporters' questions. "I have nothing to say," he said. "You can see as much as I can. All that we know is what we can see with our eyes. You can see as well as I."[77]

The archbishop's visit on Saturday, November 16, was much the same. He reached the cemetery in the late afternoon and strolled about the grounds for about an hour in the company of Joseph Walsh. He again stood silently at the grave, prayed at All Souls' Chapel and even stopped to inquire after the health of a crippled boy in a nearby car. This time in response to reporters he replied that "there is absolutely nothing to say." Then with a slight gesture he decided to add, "You may say what you wish. I must remain silent."[78]

Before he left though, O'Connell did make it known that he was very pleased at the order and the dignity that was maintained by the thousands of people filing past Patrick Power's grave. However, order, dignity, and respect did not always rule the day that autumn in Malden in 1929. "On Sunday, November 10, one of the biggest crowds I had ever seen in the cemetery was present," Walsh stated in his December 1 report. "The crowd was so great that at 4:45 p.m. I had to remove the monument from the grave to save it from destruction as the crowd had pressed two of the pedestals from under the monument."[79]

The *Boston Globe* reported that on the tenth of November, 100,000 people packed into Holy Cross. "But the removal of the tablet did not stop the rush of thousands of men, women and children to the grave and it became necessary to lock the gates of the cemetery to keep the crowd out tonight," the *Globe* reported. "A number of children were re-ported lost during the day. One gravestone was partly overturned by the crowd." The Malden police had a busy day controlling the mob. "The police detail was increased to 14 officers and they strove by shouted orders and arm persuasion to hold the throng in check."[80] The Malden Police payroll was nearly $1,000 per week that November, employing not only reserve officers, but off duty regular officers as well.[81]

While the Power tombstone was being repaired and was eventually brought back to the burial site at the end of that week, cemetery of-ficials decided to erect a fence around the grave to control the crowd. Walsh and some of his assistants worked for six hours in the dark to construct the fence before the mobs returned the next day. This was from midnight until the sun came up on the morning of Monday, No-vember 11, just one day after the stone had been removed.[82] With the site now properly protected, Holy Cross officials decided that effective immediately they would keep the grounds open twenty four hours a day to accommodate the sea of wonder seekers.[83] The fence they built was a low wooden affair with openings on either side, one for those incoming, and then one for the outgoing traffic.[84] Such measures were a constant feature during that chaotic month. The day before the fence was put up, three mounted police officers tried to reign in the crowd who three times broke through some ropes that had been stretched around the grave. Outside the gates, 35 police officers handled traffic control while inside 75 members of the Malden American Legion patrolled the grounds as women fainted, children lost their parents, and piercing prayers and screams filled the air.[85]

Using wheelbarrows teeming with fresh dirt, cemetery workers labored constantly to replace the dwindling supply of earth holding up Power's tombstone, as pilgrim after pilgrim pilfered a handful for themselves.[86] Quite likely, many visitors who took home this sacred souvenir may have believed that they had in their possession the original soil that surrounded the grave, when in fact very few individuals would have had the opportunity to sample that initial allotment of earth that first covered Power's coffin. Nevertheless, others might argue though that the originality of the dirt is not important, just the fact that at some point it covered the late priest's earthly remains, no matter at what time, or for how long.

The dirt itself and the water gathered in the chalice carved into the tombstone were the focus of many of the reported miracles during those 30 days. A detailed list of the best documented cases of these alleged wonders has been left for the appendix, but we will point out here that miracles were reported nearly every day from the time of the first published account in late October until the cemetery gates were closed in late November. Estimates have varied as to the actual number of miracles said to have taken place that autumn. Richard Bradley, director of operations for the Catholic Cemetery Association of the Archdiocese of Boston at Holy Cross Cemetery in Malden, puts the number at somewhere between 109 and 119.[87] Certainly that many names were published in local newspaper accounts of the events, but that estimate may be low considering the fact that 1 million people visited the grave. It is quite possible that scores of people may have been allegedly cured and never saw the need to publicize what happened to them, perhaps believing that such a healing was a private matter between them and God.[88] (See endnote)

Some statistics that are impossible to know but would shed some light on this matter is to find out how many of the 1 million people came seeking a cure, how many came simply out of curiosity, and how many claimed to be healed. If we knew these figures then we could determine the percentage of people who sought a miracle who claimed to have actually been cured. Unfortunately for historians there was not a census taker at the gates asking questions when people entered, and then another bean counter asking every person when they left if they were healed. Instead, we have to rely on newspaper reports, unpublished archival material, interviews, and personal recollections, all of which fall short of painting the entire picture.

It is safe to say though that not everyone came seeking a miracle, and of those that did, not everyone met with success. In fact, Boston mayor elect James M. Curley, perhaps the most high profile visitor to the gravesite (with the exception of the Archbishop), served to prove this point. He visited the cemetery on Sunday morning November 17, 1929, with his son, James Jr., at his side. He came to pray for his ailing wife, and even returned that evening with her, and her nurse, to kneel in front of the grave in a misty rainfall near dusk.[89] "It is a wonderful sight,"[90] he commented, adding that he thought his wife was progressing satisfactorily. Unfortunately though, Curley's wife passed away shortly after their trip to Holy Cross Cemetery.[91]

Despite the lack of success on the part of the mayor-elect, Curley is a good example of the intense spiritual devotion present in most pilgrims. Some seemed satisfied even without a cure. "There is reverence everywhere," said Rev. Albert E. George after spending nearly an entire day walking through the cemetery grounds and soaking in the ambiance. "The atmosphere is charged with a religious awe. It is contagious. No matter about cures. They will come anyway. But feel the devotional air here. It is thrilling and responsive to our needs."[92]

Sadly though, some visitors chose to take advantage of this. A Pennsylvania man, claiming to be crippled, boisterously exclaimed in front of the gravesite that he had been cured after years of excruciating suffering. He then made of show of discarding his crutches and passing a hat to collect money "for his trip home." However, this stranger committed a crucial oversight. His crutches and his bandages were both brand new, and had obviously not been through years of dutiful service to an invalid. The Malden police detained the man. After interviewing him they quickly determined that he was a fraud and promptly forced the "cripple" to leave the cemetery immediately.[93]

Attempts at deception were just one of the many strange aspects to the events of that fall in Malden which at times contributed to a near circus-like atmosphere. As the days stretched on, people began to complain of stolen cars, pilfered purses, and missing wallets.[94] Outside, vendors were making a steady business off photographs of Father Power, as well as hot dogs, drinks, and sandwiches, all from a line of trucks parked near the gates of the cemetery. Day after day, roads leading to those gates were jammed for miles with cars donning out of state license plates, often idling in double lines, and people on foot moving slowly into town between the vehicles. [95] License plates were spotted from Maine, New Hampshire, Vermont, Rhode Island, Connecticut, New York, Pennsylvania, New Jersey, Arizona, many Midwestern states, and most of the eastern Canadian provinces.[96] During the peak days in November, trolley cars from the Boston Elevated System ran every two minutes with commuters destined for Malden.[97]

The situation seemed to be reaching a critical mass. Cardinal O'Connell decided that it was time to step in. On Friday night, November 22, the Archdiocese of Boston released a statement to the press that read in part "the Cardinal…has decided that for the interest of all concerned the cemetery will be closed to all except funerals, beginning Monday morning (November 25), until further notice."[98]

Why did the diocese close the gates, at least temporarily? "They really wanted to cool it and they thought that the only way to do this was to close the cemetery," said Richard Bradley of the Catholic Cemetery Association. "They really wanted to kind of downplay this. The thought of miracles at the time was probably not in the real mainstream."[99]

Another reason given for the closing of the cemetery was that this was a necessary first step in the process of possible canonization for Patrick Power.[100] The reasoning went, the diocese needed time to investigate what had happened at the cemetery and would have been unable to effectively do so under the continuing strain of endless religious pilgrims visiting the shrine. As we will see, it is true that the diocese did conduct a formal investigation into the alleged miracles, but was never able to take the laborious steps required to place Patrick Power's name up for sainthood.

Still, whatever the reason, be it overreaction, fear, or the need to investigate, the cold, hard fact for many disappointed believers was that the gates were locked and there was no word on when, or if, they would reopen again. The region had just been through one of the largest concentrated outpourings of firry religious devotion in all of American history. Patrick Power had gone from an obscure country priest to a national phenomenon almost overnight and plenty of people wanted to know how, why, and more importantly if all of the bizarre tales that they had heard were in fact true. The Catholic Church in Boston wanted some answers too. So as that sacred ground in Malden began to cool, the archdiocese went about trying to answer these burning questions. So will we.

Chapter Three: Closing the Gates

William R. Marschat of Mansfield Center, MA, on November 27, 1929, praying at the entrance of Holy Cross Cemetery, two days after the gates were closed.

International Newsreel courtesy of Archdiocese of Boston Archives

When Cardinal William O'Connell closed Holy Cross Cemetery on Monday, November 25, 1929, he was assured of the fact that, at least temporarily, no more pilgrims would be visiting the grave of Father Patrick Power. The religious hysteria was over. Or was it? A tide of people was soon replaced with a torrent of letters, entreating "his Eminence" to reopen the cemetery, to make personal exceptions for individuals seeking divine help, to send information about this mysterious Patrick Power, or even to mail small pieces of the grave itself. These urgent notes poured in from the farthest reaches of the globe including Mariaco, Puerto Rico; St. Gallen, Switzerland; Chihuahua, Mexico; Eskasoni Chapel, Nova Scotia; Montreal, Canada; County Wexford, Ireland; Gaucheaue, France; and even Jamaica. People wrote to the cardinal from across the United States as well including Havre, Montana; Athens, Georgia; Los Angeles, California; Chicago, Illinois; Seattle, Washington; Jacksonville, Florida; Victoria, Texas; White Lake, South Dakota; Iowa City, Iowa; Dawson, Nebraska; Fort Wayne, Indiana; Cumberland, Maryland; Oregon City, Oregon; Philadelphia, Pennsylvania; and Cortland, New York, just to name a few.

Each author wanted something. Each letter had a request. If no response was received from the chancery (as was the case the vast majority of the time) many did not feel shy in writing again, and again, or even trying a different route. The Mayor of Boston, James M. Curley, got so many requests to intercede with the cardinal to obtain soil from the Power grave that he had a form letter ready to be mailed out to disappointed miracle seekers. "I regret exceedingly that I cannot comply with your request," the statement invariably read. "The Church authorities have forbidden the taking or distribution of earth from the grave, pending an investigation as to the cures which have been reported."[101]

Whether the letters were directed to Mayor Curley, or to Cardinal O'Connell, the men and women who wrote provided a glimpse into just how far the name and reputation of Father Power had spread. There was a great deal of hope and faith in these requests, and perhaps even a measure of naiveté. In the missives where a relic was requested, author after author seemed oblivious to the fact that there were thousands of other people also asking for soil, stone, and/or water from the grave. To have filled all such requests from these individuals would have left nothing at the gravesite except for a huge hole in the ground. Not only that, the vast majority of letters were written and addressed directly to Cardinal O'Connell. The writers assumed that he would have the time to answer their concerns personally, again seemingly unaware that countless other people might be writing to him, or that his duties as a cardinal in the Catholic Church at perhaps the most prominent archdiocese in the country might not afford him a great deal of time to answer personal mail. And yet the letters came. Call it naiveté. Call it faith. If nothing else these letters read as a magnificent testimony to the human spirit.

Some were not yet aware that the cemetery would be closing. Mrs. Francis Butler of Cleveland, Ohio, who had a crippled infant, asked O'Connell on November 24, 1929, if he "would be able to spare the time to write to me as to the authenticity of the cures" to see if it would be worthwhile to make the "sacrifice to go there." That very day in Kansas City, Kansas, Charles McDonald wrote that he "would appreciate it if the Cardinal would send me some of the earth or water from the priest's grave so as to get some relief from" the ailments that he and his wife were suffering from such as "lung, heart, and throat trouble." B. Donovan of Cincinnati, Ohio, also wrote hoping that he could help his ailing wife. "I would be willing to pay for just a handful of earth from the grave," Donovan stated on November 25, 1929. "If it cures I will advertise it all over country," he promised. The same day that Donovan was penning his request in Ohio, Mrs. Charles Fleming of Bridgeport, Connecticut, wrote to ask for either a bit "of water or earth from the grave" for her husband's upcoming throat operation.[102]

An entire "box of dirt" from the gravesite was what Mary Vincent Owens of Blacksburg, Virginia, wanted when she wrote on November 26, 1929. Mrs. Joseph Dennis from Nova Scotia, Canada, also desired a relic from the burial site, but took a more proactive approach in trying to obtain it. "I shall be very grateful if I can obtain through you some water from Father Power's grave," she wrote on April 10, 1930. "I am mailing a bottle for the purpose and I also enclosed ten cents to cover postage."[103] Simple water or dirt would not suffice for Mary Feehan of Ireland. She wanted some of the headstone itself. "I would be very thankful if you would send me a bit of the stone that is over Father Patrick Power's grave," she said in a long handwritten letter dated November 5, 1929. The piece would be used to help the "pains" in her mother's bones, she said.[104]

Many others had no interest in a relic. Instead, they wanted answers. "Is there any real truth in (the reported miracles)?" asked Mrs. F. L. Maracong of Racine, Wisconsin, on November 25, 1929. Josephine Zdrodowski from Maspeth, New York, wanted to know as well. "I am Catholic," she told O'Connell in a note also dated November 25, 1929. "I believe that you would be so kind as to let me know if these things are really true."[105] George Smith from Detroit, Michigan, saw an article about Father Power in his local newspaper, *The Detroit Times*. "Were all these people cured at once as the paper stated here?" he asked on December 29, 1929.[106] As late as 1934 the chancery still got letters which wanted an answer to this fundamental question of the truthfulness of the miracles. "Is it true that sufferers of arthritis are cured by kneeling upon this grave?" wondered Miss Hazel Leuger of Hot Springs, Arkansas, on April 26, 1934.[107]

A father and son from New Jersey who were denied entry to Holy Cross Cemetery after learning it had been closed on November 25, 1929.

International Newsreel courtesy of Archdiocese of Boston Archives

When answers were not needed, information was, even many years later. "I have been requested by the editors of a German Catholic encyclopedia to write a brief notice on the tomb of Fr. Power, of which we all heard so much some five or six years ago," wrote Professor Francis L. Betton from Marguette University in Milkwaukee, Wisconsin, on March 30, 1934. Mrs. Paul Bouchaert also wanted to know more about this mysterious priest. "I received a letter from an aunt in Belgium asking me about a Father Power..and some miracles that had been performed by him," she wrote in January 1950[108], hoping to find out more.

Yet far outnumbering these entreaties for relics, answers, and information, were the letters imploring the cardinal first to keep the cemetery open, then to reopen it, or even to ask for a special dispensation, just this once. "I ask you in the name of our Dear Lord, if I come there quietly, will you please see that I be let in?" wrote a woman from Middlefield, New York, on November 27, 1929. She had partial deafness, diabetes, and heart trouble. "I shall only stay a second but I feel I shall be healed." In a short note scribed on November 20, 1929, Mary Ida Bonanneta of New York City, "a good Catholic girl with poor eyesight," stated that "I would like to be cured." She then asked O'Connell for directions to the grave.[109]

A group of "good Catholics and working women," all from Boston-area towns, and all claiming to have been healed in some way at the Power grave, collectively sent a letter to Cardinal O'Connell on November 22, 1929. They wrote to "earnestly beg your kindly and powerful influence in keeping the gates open until at least 8 p.m. each night," so that they could visit Holy Cross Cemetery after getting out of work. Although the women included no details of their alleged healings, they all signed their names and hometowns in an accompanying document. They numbered 63 in all.[110]

Mrs. H. C. Feish of Rowena, Texas, requested that she be allowed to bring her paralyzed daughter to the gravesite. "I am very anxious to find a place where she may be cured," she wrote on November 23, 1929. Two days later in Cleveland, Ohio, Mrs. Sophia Rzonca penned a ten-page letter pleading with the cardinal to allow her to bring her ailing mother to the Power grave. "She is the only dear loving thing that we have on this earth," she said, hoping to bring an end to her mother's constant leg and breast pain. On November 26, 1929, Mrs. J. Cichan of Kulpmont, Pennsylvania, simply asked, "would you kindly let me come out there with my crippled boy to that cemetery?"[111]

Some letters were not as polite. Cardinal O'Connell also received a fair share of criticism via the daily mail. "Are you not starting something or allowing it to grow that will do more harm than good?" asked a man from Ironton, Ohio, on November 24, 1929. Other people were openly angry that the cemetery was closed. "You preach from the altar about wanting men, women and children to believe in the Catholic religion…and you have heard and read about the wonderful cures that have happened at Fr. Power's grave," wrote James L. Micheuer of Medford, Massachusetts, on November 25, 1929. "And yet you close the gates to thousands of poor unfortunate people who are only too glad and eager to ask God upon their bended knees for relief. Do you think that is consistent with your teachings?"[112]

Needless to say, the head of the Archdiocese of Boston may have felt a degree of pressure to act. After the gates of the cemetery were closed, he quickly decided to do two things. First, he would have the body of Father Patrick Power moved to a more accessible part of Holy Cross Cemetery. Second, he would authorize an investigation into the alleged miracles attributed to Father Power's intercession. That investigation and the results that it yielded are the subject of the next chapter, but right now there is a body to move.

The subject of the removal of Patrick Power's body has been shrouded in speculation, folkloric stories, and controversy over the years. Some visitors to his current resting spot may not even be aware that he was originally buried somewhere else in the cemetery, and that the 1929 miracles attributed to his intercession are not associated with what is now his second resting spot. Power's remains currently lie on the western side of South Cedar Avenue, near the main entrance to Holy Cross Cemetery at 175 Broadway in Malden. This is the so-called "Monument Avenue." The location of his original burial spot is not widely known. An exhaustive, patient, search of the archives at Holy Cross Cemetery, conducted by the current staff, yielded no record of the location of Power's original grave. Is it possible that diocesan officials in 1929 wished to erase from history the location of this controversial piece of real estate? We will see in the next chapter that the archdiocese understandably demonstrated a reluctance to hype the events in Malden in its final report on the matter. This fact is also demonstrated by the refusal of the chancery to mail out samples of soil or water from the grave to people who had requested these relics. To their credit, they were simply not going to run a mail order religious clearinghouse for the miraculous. Thus, is the absence of records at the Holy Cross Cemetery archives more evidence of this desire to "cool it" (in the appropriate words of Richard Bradley)?

The original location of Father Power's gravesite at Holy Cross Cemetery, now an empty space between the graves of Rev. Timothy Hannigan and Rev. Thomas Cusack. This location is on South Oak Avenue, east side, fifth lot, in the so-called "Religious Lot," or "Clergymen's Lot."

Photo by Tammy Koerner

More questions through the years have also surrounded the re-moval of the body. Were Power's remains actually re-interred on South Cedar Avenue, or was his body left at the original site? If this was the case, was it done to see if the miracles would continue at the new site without the body there, perhaps indicating that people were fabricat-ing their miraculous stories? Incidentally, this would not have proven anything. Miracles attributed to the intercession of a holy person have been known to occur anywhere, and are absolutely not necessarily tied to a specific geographical location.[113] (See endnote) We will see in the final chapter for example that in November 1929 a man who never even left his hospital in Havana, Cuba, was likely cured of leprosy by Power's intercession, this testified to by a Catholic nun.

All of these questions can be put to an end with a single docu-ment. This lengthy statement not only proves that Power's body was removed, but that all of his remains were placed at his current resting spot. Because all of the remains were moved, it also demonstrates that the cardinal had no ulterior motive in transferring the body. Appar-ently the primary motive was probably just a practical one. If the grave was moved to a more open area with an iron fence around it (which is what happened), then there would be little chance that large numbers of pilgrims could damage nearby headstones. This was the problem with the original site. It was too close to other grave markers, and these tombstones had been overrun by the mass of pilgrims seeking to reach the Power grave. Also, the new location would provide easier access for potential pilgrims.

The existence of this document, found in the chancery archives, also proves that the diocese did not want to erase the location of Power's original gravesite because this report states exactly where he was originally buried. If the Cardinal wanted the location forgotten, this document would have been destroyed. In fact, it probably would have been the first thing on the hit list.

The current location of Father Power's gravesite at Holy Cross Cemetery on South Cedar Avenue.

Photo by Tammy Koerner

This important piece of our collective puzzle was generated in response to the following letter directed to Father Patrick H. Walsh at St. Joseph's Church in Malden. Rev. F. A. Burke, chancellor of the Archdiocese of Boston (second only to O'Connell in the diocese) sent this letter to Walsh to ask him to participate in a very delicate matter. The letter, dated December 2, 1929, read exactly as follows.

> His Eminence, the Cardinal, directs me to say that he wishes you to confer with Mr. E. J. O'Connell regarding the removal of the body of Rev. Patrick Power. His Eminence further directs me to convey to you the following instructions: He has appointed you Notary and you are to draw up a document stating that the body of Rev. Patrick Power, buried at such a time, was exhumed from such a place, and reburied in such a place, and this is to be signed by you and Mr. Joseph Walsh. The coffin is to be taken into the Chapel and opened and is to be certified just how the remains look. The body must be remained intact. It is to be put into another box which is to be closed up and sealed in such a way that any tampering with it must be detected. Very sincerely yours, F.A. Burke.[114]

By January 8, 1930, Burke was given his answer to forward to Cardinal O'Connell, and through this same letter we will now have our answers to the questions posed above as well.

> This is to certify that we the undersigned do hereby testify and do solemnly swear under oath, that we were present at the exhuming of the body of Rev. Patrick J. Power, buried December 10, 1869, in the 5th lot east side on South Oak Avenue and that the remains were removed from said grave at All Soul's Chapel where the remains were examined by us.
>
> The remains were then re-interred to grave on westerly side of South Cedar Avenue in front of All Soul's Chapel.
>
> We further testify we found the remains as they were uncovered in the grave No. 5 in the so-called Religious Lot fronting on South Oak where he was buried on December 10, 1869.

The skull, pelvis, vertebrae, thigh, shin bones, and ribs were clean and sound, other pieces of small bones presumably of the feet and hands were carefully collected and placed with the other remains in a sealed casket. The coffin in which the body of the Rev. Patrick Power was buried was gone to decay, only a small part of the bottom of the coffin remained, coffin handles, name plate on coffin found in grave of Rev. Patrick Power in Holy Cross Cemetery in so called Religious Lot grave No. 5 fronting on South Oak Avenue, Friday, December 13, 1929, at 1:30 p.m.

The piece of plate recovered is in the state of corrosion. It measures in longest part 4 inches from end to end, the short part 3 inches across. The plate is composed of either silver or pewter plated. The words in raised letters Rev. Patrick died Dec. aged 25 is all that is on the remains of the plate and might be brought out clearer by cleaning.

(signed)
Patrick H. Walsh, P. P.
David W. Lenehan, P. P.
George A. Gately, C. C.
Edward J. O'Connell, Supt. Cemetery
Middlesex, S. S.
State of Massachusetts
Subscribed before me this date
Joseph J. Walsh
Justice of the Peace
January 8, 1930[115]

Rev. Patrick H. Walsh was the pastor of St. Joseph's Church in Malden, and chaplain of the cemetery. Rev. David W. Lenehan was the pastor of Sacred Heart Church in Malden. Rev. George A. Gately was a prelate at St. Joseph's Church. Edward J. O'Connell was the superintendent of Holy Cross Cemetery, and Joseph J. Walsh was assistant superintendent as well a local justice of the peace. Local newspaper reports also placed several other individuals at the scene, including Captain John Aylward of the Malden Police Department, Sergeant James Ryan of the Massachusetts State Police Department, two unnamed laymen, and three gravediggers.[116]

Several observations can be made from this key letter. Obviously, it provides us with the original location of Power's grave which we find out here was on South Oak Avenue, east side, fifth lot, in the so-called "Religious Lot," or "Clergymen's Lot." This was only about 75 yards away from the subsequent burial location where Power's grave is today. The letter also tells us that the remains definitely were dug up, taken to All Soul's Chapel, removed from their coffin, placed in a new casket, and then re-interred at the present location on South Cedar Avenue. This was sworn to by the five men who witnessed it. Newspaper reports provide us with the further details that the new casket for Father Power was bronze instead of pine (as the old one had been), and that now he was buried in a bevy of concrete instead of dirt, with a six foot high fence around his gravestone.[117]

A further bit of evidence to confirm the complete removal of the body is provided by Richard Bradley, director of operations at the Catholic Cemetery Association of the Archdiocese of Boston. He has seen a document similar to the one recorded above, but was signed by the actual gravediggers who unearthed the remains of Father Power on December 13, 1929. These men essentially confirmed in the document that they had removed the coffin, witnessed the transfer of remains, and then reburied the new casket in the current location on South Cedar. "When I first started here about thirty years ago I saw a hand-written paper in the safe," said Bradley in a 2005 interview. "It was all in chronological order" giving the exact time of exhuming and reburial of Father Power. At the bottom of the document "all of the gravediggers signed it and swore to it."[118] A patient, thorough, search by the Holy Cross staff for this rare gem unfortunately yielded no results, but Bradley's memory of its contents were detailed enough to warrant mention of its existence.[119] The gravediggers document along with the Walsh letter mentioned above together put to rest some speculation on the subject of where Father Power used to be buried, and if all of him in fact made it over to South Cedar.

The letter also raises a question in my own mind. Quite often when a holy person's remains are uncovered, miracles of incorruptibility crop up. The Incorruptibles are the group of holy and sainted men and women of the Catholic Church whose bodies resisted various stages of decay after their deaths. Sometimes these bodies would stay fresh for months, or even years at a time. In other instances, corpses would be accompanied by beautiful aromas after rigor mortis, and even when dug up. There are many instances of this phenomenon. St. Teresa of Avila (1515 – 1582) is probably the most famous example. When she died at Alba de Tormes in Spain it is said that a wondrous smell came forth from her body, and that later when one of her confessors had her grave opened, the body looked vibrant and new, and the scent of lilies filled the air.[120]

And yes, even Father Nelson Baker can be looked at as part of the tradition of incorruptibility. When his remains were unearthed in 1999 and moved to Our Lady of Victory Basilica, three vials of his blood that were buried with him in 1936 were found to still be fluid, and furthermore to possess active red blood cells. In other words, his blood had inexplicably resisted decomposition for just over 60 years. Interestingly, at this point we can add yet another parallel between Baker and Power. In each case at the point of approximately six decades after each man died, their remains were unearthed and moved to a second, final resting spot. Furthermore, in both instances this was done in part to accommodate the large number of people visiting their respective graves asking for a miracle.

In recent years, the Vatican has moved away from miracles of incorruptibility. In the 1980s and 1990s, many of the incorruptible bodies (not all) were allowed to be examined scientifically, and some were found to have been put through various stages of preservation such as stitching and embalming. This was an embarrassment to the Church because in the past the Vatican had allowed many such cases to be used as one of the required miracles for sainthood. Add this public relations problem to the fact that the Catholic Church bestows credibility only on complete, "100 percent" miracles, and you have a phenomenon which quickly fell out of favor.

However, in 1929 incorruptibility was not yet out of vogue in the Catholic world. In all likelihood the Archdiocese of Boston probably wanted to see just what kind of condition these apparently miraculous remains were in, and if they could be said to be incorruptible. Was it possible that Father Power could have resisted decomposition, especially since the diocese had a body on their hands which had lived for only 25 years? We documented earlier that Father Burke specifically directed Father Walsh in his instructional letter that "the coffin is to be taken into the Chapel and opened and is to be certified just how the remains look." We stated above that the body was being moved for practical reasons, but is it possible that the diocese wanted to exhume the remains to check for incorruptibility as well? In looking at Burke's directive to Walsh it certainly seems that this subject may have weighed on their minds.

It should also be noted that the remains were reported to be "clean and sound." We do not wish to make too much of this statement other than to say that it is frustrating that this is the only extant document which describes the remains of Father Power as they looked some 60 years after his death. Yet we still cannot help but wonder, just what was the meaning of "clean and sound?" It was probably nothing. Or was it?

Certainly the local media did not think it was insignificant. Local newspapers were not hesitant to mention that according to their sources "those present when the body of the priest was exhumed were reported to have expressed their astonishment at the condition of the body and casket,"[121] and that "those who saw the skeleton remarked at the state of preservation after its six decades in the earth."[122] Power's expensive white vestments in which he was buried were also reported to be in a perfect state of preservation, a fact not noted in the chancery report on the matter.[123]

Yet perhaps most intriguing of all is a curious weather anomaly that took place on the day of the removal of the body. December 13, 1929, was a curious day for Mother Nature. Rain and wind accompanied the transfer of Power's remains, as well as a heavy fog, something rarely seen in December. In fact, the cover of fog may have been the reason the diocese chose to move Power on that particular day. In any event, the fog lifted just as Father Power's pine box came out of the earth, allowing the gathered crowds at the gates to see this private ritual at the pivotal moment.[124]

For many this would be the only glimpse that they would get of the grave until the following year. During the time when Holy Cross Cemetery was closed to the public, visitors were periodically let in for funerals or to visit private graves (such as on New Year's Day 1930),[125] but not allowed to visit the old Power gravesite, or even the new burial location. This did not change until April 1930 when Holy Cross Cemetery was finally reopened to the public. No official ceremony took place when the large iron gates were finally swung back again and the patrolling Massachusetts State Troopers left for good. However, a few new rules accompanied the reopening. The cemetery was now open from 9 a.m. to 5 p.m. on weekdays and 1 p.m. to 5 p.m. on Sundays. No longer would pilgrims be permitted to visit until sunset, or even overnight. No loitering about the grave would be allowed, and any large crowds which might form would immediately be broken up by the Malden Police Department.

"We will not allow the huge crowds of last November around the grave, nor will we let persons form long lines like last fall,"[126] stated Superintendent E. J. O'Connell. For the most part he did not need to worry about this. For a short while, Sundays were marginally heavy in volume at the new grave, but the crowds never again approached their November levels. The first large crowd was on Sunday, April 6, 1930, when between 6,000 and 7,000 interested parties visited the new grave in a "dignified and orderly" fashion.[127] On Sunday, April 20, about 5,000 individuals visited the new Power grave[128] and two weeks later in May, 6,000 pilgrims made the trip to Malden. Yet by the time Memorial Day 1930 rolled around, all of those who wanted to view the new burial location had apparently done so. The *Boston Herald* reported that on that day thousands of people came to Holy Cross to tend to the graves of loved ones, "but only a handful visiting the cemetery paused at" the Power grave.[129]

Even though the public may have started to lose interest in this long dead Irish priest, the archdiocese of Boston had not. On the day that the cemetery reopened to the public, one of the first visitors who approached the grave was a man who came unannounced, a man who chose to stop at the new grave and remain in private prayer. This man was none other than Cardinal William O'Connell. Through it all he had remained silent. Through it all he had allowed no official statement, nor provided any of his own. Yet while the gates were closed, he authorized an investigation into just how credible these alleged miracles were. During these winter months, the archdiocese was busily carrying out an inquiry into the miracles attributed to the intercession of Father Power. What this investigation turned up may have been one of the reasons why the diocese has never officially endorsed or rejected what happened in Malden in 1929. In essence, the report turned up more questions than it could possibly have answered. It is the subject of our next chapter.

Chapter Four: The Official Miracles

The question was simple really. Were the miracles real? The Archdiocese of Boston wanted an answer to this question, and because they wanted an answer who better to investigate these claims than the very priests who worked in the parishes where the alleged cures came from? With this in mind, beginning in late November, 1929, scores of prelates throughout the archdiocese began to receive the following letter from the Rev. O. L. Chaput, assistant to Father F. A. Burke, chancellor of the Archdiocese of Boston. "Will you kindly investigate the case of (a particular individual from that parish) who was reported as having been cured after a visit to the grave in Malden? If you judge this case worthy of an official inquiry please notify the Rt. Rev. Vicar General."[130]

The priests contacted were swift in responding and usually answered back to Chaput by the end of December, or early January 1930, at the latest. What the investigations yielded was as varied as the cures that they were probing. On December 27, 1929, Pastor Michael Delaney at St. Patrick's Parish in Natick was cautious in his final report, stating that for the inquiry he conducted he "found a slight improvement which may only be coincidental to the visit to the shrine. This possibility of mere natural improvement however places the case outside of the sphere of the miraculous."[131]

The parish staff at St. Anthony's in Revere offered a similarly mixed bag in their examination of a local deaf and dumb woman. They concluded in a December 18, 1929, letter that while it was true that "after praying at the grave of Father Power's she talked fluently and heard as well for about 10 minutes," but since that time "has not spoken at all fluently."[132]

In an exhaustive, detailed missive penned on December 14, 1929, Father Albert Jacobbe of St. Polycarp Parish pressed his case for what he considered to be a miraculous cure of a nine year old girl "born with her right arm paralyzed and pressed against her breast. Dr. E. H. Robbins…was the attending physician. (The girl) was unable to move the fingers, hand or arm in any way." She was taken to Children's Hospital in Boston when she was a month old for treatment and examination. "These periodic treatments continued for years with no noticeable improvement," Jacobbe wrote.

Then in early November 1929 she made two visits to the grave of Father Power. "On the night of her second visit to the grave, while at home, her father sprinkled her with water brought from the grave of Fr. Power. (The girl) then raised her right arm over head. Since then she has recovered the use of her fingers." Jacobbe also wrote that "she can write with her right hand, grasp objects, move the arm up and down, but is unable to straighten it out to its full length. The child's mother "brought (her daughter) into the living room and the girl proved her ability to use her right arm in the above mentioned ways."[133] Jacobbe was convinced that this particular set of circumstances presented evidence of a true miraculous healing worthy of further inquiry.

Other priests offered outright rejections of cases that they had researched. Father Timothy A. Curtin of Sacred Heart Parish at Newton Center was unequivocal in his assessment. He stated on December 29, 1929, that in his estimation the child he visited "was not improved in the least by the visit to the grave. Her condition is the same as it has been for years."[134]

Father John Gorham found much the same in the case of a Woburn boy from his St. Charles Parish. "There seems to be nothing worthy of an official inquiry in this case. I have seen the child and his parents," Gorham wrote on December 16, 1929. "The boy is ailing since birth with some brain trouble which causes paralysis of his left side and lower limbs." The boy was brought to the grave on November 11, and then again the following Tuesday, and Wednesday, each time having soil from the grave rubbed on him. "After these visits to the priest's grave they noticed no change in the condition of the child."[135]

Results were also disappointing for Assistant Pastor David V. Fitzgerald at St. Joseph's Church in Somerville. He wrote to Father Chaput on December 16 that further inquiry into the alleged cure in his parish "should be cancelled, as the report of his cure has been found, on investigation, to be false."[136]

After all of the priests reported to the chancery with their findings, the diocese was faced with the task of making some sense out of what had been uncovered. In the final analysis, the archdiocese ended up investigating thirty-five cases. A heretofore unpublished summary was written based upon these 35 separate inquiries, and then issued to Cardinal O'Connell. This report was unsigned but we will assume that it was penned by Rev. Chaput who was not only at the receiving end of nearly all of the correspondence from the parish investigations, but he also headed up the entire inquiry process almost single-handedly. The author of the report insists in the introduction that he had conducted a "painstaking and careful examination" of the alleged miracles that had come to his attention. This statement could only really apply to Father Chaput. No other person was as close to the "examination" as him. The reverend then proceeded in his introduction to divide the miracles into five separate categories. "1st – A miraculous cure testified by physicians, 2nd – What appears to be a miraculous cure but unsupported by testimony of physicians, 3rd – Cases in which there is no doubt a very great improvement, 4th – Cases in which there is considerable improvement, 5th – Cases in which there is some or little improvement."[137]

The sole member of category number one was a 17 year old girl by the name of Laura Moody from Dorchester, Massachusetts. We can use her name here because her identity was reported in local newspapers during late 1929.[138] According to the chancery's final report she "was afflicted with what is known as a poker back which was encased in a cast. The physician who attended her at the City Hospital and the physician who treated her at home testify that in their belief there is an absolute cure which cannot be anything other than a miracle." Moody "now goes about with no appearance of any previous ailment."[139]

But the trail does not run cold there. The information we have about Laura Moody extends beyond the chancery's report. We also have at our disposal the original testimony given by her two physicians, providing us with the entire story behind what the archdiocese considered to be their most credible miracle. Each doctor submitted lengthy, exhaustive letters, pouring out all that they knew about her recovery. A Brookline doctor who had seen his former patient in the newspaper wrote to Cardinal O'Connell on November 30, 1929, to voice his conviction that Moody had been miraculously cured.[140] However, he asked at that time that his letter not be published, therefore we will continue to respect his wishes here.

The other doctor in question was Edward Leonard of Dorchester who wrote to the chancery on March 7, 1930. He began by plainly stating that "this is to certify that the cure of Laura Moody is a miracle." During the time that he treated her he "found her condition to be that of acute tonsillitis, later developing into septicemia," a disease of the blood stream. Leonard advised her to be treated at the Boston City Hospital, where she stayed for several months. "She was discharged to her home as incurable. On her arrival I was asked by her aunt to take the case. Examining her I found her left leg in a brace extending from hip to foot. Removing the brace I found the knee very tender to touch, limited motion, and very painful even if passively moved." Leonard wrote that the hip was in the same condition and that Moody's "leg and foot were cold and hypersensitive to the touch. A body cast had also been applied, extending from the neck to below the hips...Examining her back, I found the spinal column stiff." The Dorchester doctor then related that when he tried to remove her body cast, it was so painful that he had to administer a potent painkiller. He tried the same approach a month later and ended up with the same outcome. "Two days prior to the trip to Father Power's grave, the same procedure was done with the same results. On this occasion I advised returning to the hospital for a new cast to further her comfort."

Moody decided not to do this. Instead, she opted for a visit to Holy Cross Cemetery, hoping for the best. "Following her return from Father Power's grave (I did not know of this intention to visit the grave) I was called to see her," Leonard wrote. "I found her walking about the home, excited, but seemingly normal in every respect. I then examined her and could find no traces of a poker back or an imperfect leg." Leonard found that Moody had "no tenderness or stiffness, was able to bend her back, touch her toes, could raise her left leg and bend it as well as she could the right. I examined her five or six days later and she was just as good as the day she visited the grave of Father Power." The physician then noted that "this statement is written months following the cure of Miss Moody and I have recently seen her and find her in excellent health. I am finally convinced that medical science had nothing to do with the cure of Laura Moody, that in my opinion it is a miracle." Leonard felt such conviction about this case that he even had his letter signed and sealed by an official notary.[141] Such testimony makes the Moody case an easy fit for a category one miracle.

The Moody case was also detailed by a reporter by the name of Grattan Kerans for the *Catholic Record* on November 29, 1929. Kerans interviewed Moody and her doctors directly and scribed a lengthy report on the remarkable series of events which surrounded this woman. According to this journalist, Moody became ill with tonsillitis on October 14, 1928. As her condition worsened into septicaemia, Dr. Leonard then advised her to go to Boston City Hospital. "During the whole period of her confinement in the hospital, and for the eight weeks and five days after her discharge – thirteen months – she did not walk," Kerans stated. "At home, as in the hospital, she remained in bed, except for intervals when she sat in a wheelchair." Walking was impossible for her. "I tried many times to walk," Moody said. Just weeks before her visit to Malden she tried to make an attempt to use her legs. "I lifted myself out of the chair, but I fell on the floor and couldn't get up. My aunt found me after about an hour."

Moody also gave to the *Catholic Record* a complete account of her trip to the Power grave. "When we got to the cemetery...my back was paining me very much. The pain grew worse as they carried me from the car to the grave. When they let me down by the grave I couldn't kneel," she told the reporter. At this point she reached down to touch the slab, but her back was in such "agony" that she could not pray. "My cousin and the strange man who helped him carry me from the car lifted me back a foot or two. I fainted. When I was myself again I was in the car. All at once I knew that I could walk and I wanted to try."

Moody then began stretching her feet towards the open car door next to her. "I put my feet under me. I could stand. Then I stepped to the ground. My cousin was holding me but I didn't need his help. I could walk. I started back to the grave. My cousin and aunt let me walk between them. When I got to the grave the people were excited. I just knelt down and prayed." The group of three then walked to All Soul's Chapel where Moody removed her cast and left it with the other artifacts gathered there. The trio then went back home and proceeded to call Dr. Leonard. When he arrived he could not believe what he saw. "He walked from the hall way (where he saw her standing) to a chair in the living room and sat down. He seemed very much astonished," Moody said. "After a few minutes he examined me and said I was all right."

One of the surgeons at Boston City Hospital who may have briefly examined Moody stated that the cause of her paralysis was "hysteria." Another doctor at the same hospital, Harold Dana, judged that Moody was only there because she had a psychological "habit of invalidism." Dr. Leonard, the physician who had the most extensive contact with Moody, vehemently denied these assertions as baseless and misinformed conjectures founded on incomplete and inaccurate assumptions. His detailed response to these accusations, given to Kerans, is worth quoting here at length to demonstrate how intimately familiar he was with this case and how Leonard logically arrived at the conclusion that there could be no medical explanation for Laura Moody's sudden recovery.

> At the beginning there was septicaemia due to tonsillitis. This affected her spine and the bones of her legs. Before she left the hospital last September one of the physicians there, speaking to me on the telephone, declared that only one of two things could be done for the girl – either commit her to an institution for the incurables or send her back home.
>
> After her return from the hospital I removed the cast and examined her searchingly. She had what is called 'poker back.' There was anchylosis, that is fusion of the vertebrae. Of that

there is no shadow of doubt in my mind. There was only one 'open spot' in her spine. That was in the small of the back. She could bend that part of her spine slightly, but even that much only with difficulty and great pain. Her mental condition was at all times normal. She was distinctly not neurotic. Moreover, she was anxious to walk and made attempts to do so. On one occasion, at her entreaty, I removed the cast so that she might try to move about. She suffered excruciatingly and I had to replace the cast.

There is no provision for the treatment of mental cases at the Boston City Hospital. She was there ten months as a medical and surgical patient. There was never a hint that her condition was psychological. I don't believe that her recovery can be attributed to psychological influences.

My own conviction was, after close study of Miss Moody's case, that she was incurable and that she would remain a cripple for life...I was unable to speak when Miss Moody herself came to the door and greeted me. I was compelled to sit down till I recovered. There was no limitation of movement in her spine, her arms, or legs, no soreness, no symptom of any physical or mental trouble...

Even if Miss Moody had experienced a delusion of illness and helplessness, her failure to walk for fourteen months, the long confinement of her body in a nearly rigid plaster cast and her mental distress would have produced physical effects that would remain for some time after her psychological attitude had changed. She would have shown debility and enfeeblement of muscles, for example. She could hardly be expected to walk and be perfectly normal in all respects within two hours after such a purely psychological change. My examination revealed no evidences of physical weakness or of any other impairment.

The personal observations of Kerans seemed to corroborate the above analysis given by Leonard. "My first – and last – impression of Miss Moody was that she was of sound health, physically and mentally.

Indeed I came in the course of the interview to regard her as above the average in intelligence," the *Catholic Record* reporter stated. Upon the request of the journalist, Moody touched her toes several times without bending her knees, bowed backwards and forwards, and leaned sideways. "All this she did without any visible sign of difficulty or distress. She said she felt no stiffness or soreness in any joint."[142]

Thus we can add this detailed analysis obtained by Grattan Kerans to the chancery analysis, and to the two original letters written by Moody's doctors. When taken as a whole it is easy to see why the diocese felt comfortable in classifying this as a type one miracle. The mountain of available evidence makes it hard to deny, but it also spoils us in a sense. As we will see, a variety of sources for a single reported miracle are rare indeed.

As for Laura Moody, according to her cousin Irene McGravey, Moody stayed healthy the rest of her life, and entered a Baltimore convent after finishing high school. She passed away there in 1995, but not before serving the Church for many years as Sister Mary Patrice, a name she took to honor Father Patrick Power.[143]

Just as in the first classification level with the Moody narrative, only one person was placed in the second category as well, this time a 20 year old woman from Malden named Florence Coughlin[144] "whose right leg was useless from the time she was 2 years old as a result of infantile paralysis." She endured five operations at the Massachusetts

General Hospital, "but was obliged to wear a brace. She now walks without a brace and with but a slight limp. Her family testifies to the extraordinary improvement in her case." So far so good, except that when Coughlin made the decision to go to the cemetery in the hope that she would be cured, she did so against the advice of her physicians who had scheduled another surgery for her. She left behind jilted doctors who then refused to talk about her case, and a staff who told her not to come back.[145]

The above case was brought to the attention of the diocese through a letter written by a parishioner at the Sacred Heart Parish in Malden where this young woman with infantile paralysis had attended church. Although it was not included in the final report, this note does provide us with some further details about the case that were not mentioned in Chaput's summary. In this letter, the parishioner wrote that "they never could cure her leg, which was operated on five times. During all this time she was using a brace on the left leg. Parts of bone were taken from one part and applied to the other on the same leg." The letter stated that when Florence Coughlin was scheduled for yet another operation at Massachusetts General Hospital, she and her family decided that instead of the surgery they would "see if Father Power could do anything for her. She went each day (to the grave) and on her third visit declared she was cured and asked to have the brace removed. She was really cured and on the following Sunday walked down the aisle of the church like other people and bent both knees for receiving our Lord at the altar rail. She has never used a brace or cane since her cure."[146]

Seven alleged cures made the cut for category number three. The first was a five year old boy who suffered from infantile paralysis, unable to use his head, or his legs, "one of which was to every appearance without circulation of blood," and a spine covered in "large lumps." The Chancery's final report stated that the boy "now has full control of his head, the lumps on his back have disappeared, (and he) can use both legs and is beginning to walk." Not only that, "the circulation of blood in the leg which previously appeared to be without circulation is now very evident." Disappointingly though, medical evidence for this alleged miracle was not obtained from the relevant doctors. "I was unable to secure the testimony of physicians in this case in as much as the step-mother stated that the doctors at the Children's Hospital laughed at her."[147]

The second case for category number three was of a 26 year old Malden woman named Helen Hunt[148] who had been a cripple for ten years and was "totally unable to help herself," according to the chancery report. In fact, during the three months prior to her visit to the Power shrine, she had been confined to her bed. After visiting the grave she was able to walk "around with a slight shuffle," an "extraordinary improvement" testified to by the investigating prelates and her family. Hunt died on January 13, 1932, from a "baffling form of sleeping sickness,"[149] according to her obituary. When reports of her cure first circulated many newspapers printed a photo of Hunt walking at the burial site with a transfixed, frightened gaze upon her face.[150]

Occupying slot number three was an Arlington, Massachusetts, woman who apparently experienced only partial convalescence after her visit to the grave. She had previously been unable to walk due to a club foot that had developed after an automobile accident, but "is now able to walk with a slight limp and the ankle is just a trifle swollen." Each physician "testified that there is no doubt of extraordinary improvement," but they "do not care to state that they feel that the case is a miraculous cure."

Fourth in line was Samuel Sidman,[151] a 20 year old Jewish man from Dorchester, Massachusetts. For many years he was without the use of his right leg after he sustained severe head injuries during a car crash, forcing him to rely on crutches. "He now has discarded the crutches and is seeking improvement." The only supporting testimony that the archdiocese could garner in this case though was from the man's brother who testified to "the wonderful improvement after (his brother's) visit to the grave."[152]

Yet another crippled Jewish Dorchester man confined to crutches was the fifth subject for the third category. This time though the improvement was thus far incomplete after making the pilgrimage to Holy Cross Cemetery. "He has discarded the crutches since his visit to the grave and uses a cane, but expects to discard this soon owing to his constant improvement…His family testifies to the extraordinary improvement." Partial healing was also the case with a 35 year old Roxbury, Massachusetts, man whose right leg had been crippled since the age of seven due to infantile paralysis. "He now goes without the brace although walking with a slight limp."[153]

The seventh and final member of category number three was a ten year old Chelsea girl by the name of Madeline MacFarlane[154] who suffered from a useless left leg until her visit to the Malden cemetery. The chancery report stated that she "had a definite pathological condition of the left pelvis, resulting in lameness of the left leg. After visiting the cemetery her lameness disappeared."[155] This case was apparently brought to the attention of the diocese by Joseph Walsh, the assistant superintendent at Holy Cross. In his December 1, 1929, report to the chancery (discussed in Chapter 2) he recounted how this story came to his attention. He stated that MacFarlane had visited the cemetery on November 9 with her grandmother, and that her left leg had been paralyzed from the hip down for over two years.

> The little girl after saying her prayers at the grave, walked away without a limp. The grandmother, overjoyed, came to me and informed me of the cure. I asked her if a doctor had been treating the little girl. She informed me that there had been. I asked her to bring a note from the doctor stating that the child had recovered. On November 10, the grandmother gave me an affidavit signed by (the family doctor), which at this time is in the possession of the cemetery.[156]

The chancery's final report allowed for only three entries to the fourth class, designated as cases with "considerable improvement." First on the list was a Dorchester teenager with a stiff, unbendable ankle which "she now bends without any trouble…Her father testifies as to her improvement." Second was an 18 year old teenager from Everett, Massachusetts, born paralyzed from the waist down, but "now goes about considerably without the aid of crutches, although he shuffles when walking." The last member of this category was a six year old suffering from infantile paralysis which "affected his right arm and both legs. He was not able to sit without support. Now he sits without support, bends his legs and raises his arms to his shoulder. His mother and grandmother testify of the improvement."[157]

The fifth and final category of healings attributed to the intercession of Father Power, as stated in the chancery's final report, had only two examples. First up was a three year old boy from Mattapoisett, Massachusetts, named Eugene Reynolds.[158] He suffered from infantile paralysis. His mother "stated that the muscles of the legs appear to be softening and responding to treatment." Second and last was a nine year old girl with a paralyzed right arm from Somerville, Massachusetts. "She was treated continuously at the Children's Hospital with no noticeable improvement. Since her visit to the grave, she raises her right arm over her head, has recovered the use of her fingers and can write and grasp objects with her right hand."[159] This was the same case mentioned above that had been investigated at St. Polycarp Parish by Father Albert Jacobbe.

A postscript to the report stated that "of the remaining 20 or so cases which were investigated, I was unable to find anyone at home or any evidence of interest. I also have six letters stating that the person referred to has been helped either by a visit to the grave or by application either of earth or water taken from the grave." Chaput stated that it was difficult to obtain more medical evidence because "most of the people reporting cures had not seen a doctor for years, went intermittently to hospitals, or found that not much credence was placed by the hospital doctors in their reported improvement."

The reverend also added that most of the individuals in question "testified that in so far as they know, neither nervousness nor imagination played any part in their altered state." Chaput summarized his report by concluding that "it seems as though there is one miraculous cure, one that at least borders on miraculous, and several which show extraordinary improvement."[160]

Although there is no date on the document, if we assume that it was authored by Father Chaput it must have been issued before July 1930, when the reverend died. This timetable makes sense given that the priests in question wrapped up their individual parish inquiries within weeks, if not days, of receiving their instructions from the archdiocese in late 1929. It would then be just a matter of collating the results into a summary suitable for the cardinal, to make the process complete.

Placing the report in 1930 is also confirmed by examining one additional clue in it. The case of Madeline MacFarlane, the seventh and final member of category number three, serves to prove this point. The chancery report placed her age as ten years old.[161] However, we know that the *Boston Globe* reported her as being nine years old in a 1929 article.[162] Therefore, logically, since the chancery report stated that this Chelsea girl was ten, it must have been written the following year when she turned that age.

The report has some weaknesses. Well over one hundred people in 1929 claimed to be miraculously healed by Father Patrick Power. Of all these people, the archdiocese chose to investigate only 35 individuals. As we saw in the second chapter, as is documented in the appendix, and as we will examine in the next chapter, there are scores of cases where individuals claimed to be completely cured, cases which were not included in the chancery's final report. Why not investigate or include these? One might point out that the cases may not have come to the attention of the diocese as yet. A fair point, but it is also a point which argues for a more patient approach with deeper digging and longer waiting to see if more cases surfaced.

Even the ones brought to the attention of the diocese did not always get the attention that they deserved. Why not investigate the six letters that Chaput mentioned in the postscript, of people claiming to be helped by water or earth from the grave? Why not go back to the houses where no one answered the door? Why not call and/or write to them to get information if a personal visit failed? Why not be more persistent? The report seems a bit hurried and incomplete. Miraculous investigations conducted by the Vatican often take years to complete. Judgments are not passed down until many investigators and theologians take a long look at a case and interview scores of witnesses. In the case of the archdiocese's investigation, inquiries were often wrapped up in days, with usually only one or two people looking into the matter, often falling to interview medical personnel, or to do follow up research. More time should have been given to flesh out incomplete inquiries, regardless of any self imposed deadlines to wrap up and issue a report.

Even the self imposed classification system used in the report can be questioned. Take for example the case investigated by Father Albert Jacobbe at St. Polycarp Parish. Father Jacobbe wrote to the chancery about a girl who could now use her right arm for the first time in her life. He witnessed this with his own eyes and interviewed the excited parents about this clearly remarkable event. He then wrote in to the chancery about his findings and recommended further inquiry. This was clearly a case where, with some time, supporting testimony could have been garnered from the Children's Hospital where the girl had gone for many years to be unsuccessfully treated. Instead, no supporting medical testimony was included or mentioned in the final report, even if to discount the alleged miracle. Instead, this very promising case, which may have been a clear example of a class one miracle, was instead the last case mentioned in the lowest classification level.

The Father Jacobbe case is not the weakest part of Chaput's summary however. In classification level three, the reverend selected as his third example the story of an Arlington, Massachusetts, woman whom he said had experienced only a partial healing of her foot. Fortunately, we have a great deal more information about this case, including the original letter from the woman which alerted the diocese of the alleged miracle, and two letters from her physicians. Each of them reveals a story that is much more intricate than the report indicated.

The woman submitted a lengthy narrative to the chancery on November 29, 1929, detailing a series of events which began in the Canadian province where Father Power was educated. "On August 23, 1929, about 16 miles this side of Quebec City, my husband and I met with an automobile accident," she said. "I sustained quite a serious injury to my foot and ankle." Her doctor said she had "an out and out dislocation with complete tearing of all tendons, ligaments, nerves and blood vessels and all circulation was completely cut off at the ankle."[163]

Her condition remained the same until her visit to Malden in late 1929. "On Monday, November 4, 1929, I was taken from my bed to the grave of Rev. Fr. Power. They rested me on the stone slab a few moments, while I prayed, and then they carried me back to the car." In the car she began to move her damaged foot, and then stood alone "without any pain." The next day she began extensive walking, again without any pain, which shocked the nurse who was attending to her at home. "She got frightened when she saw me without my crutches, but I told her I didn't need them. I could walk."

As we noted above, the woman also submitted supporting documentation from her two doctors. The first was from Dr. M. L. Messler of Cambridge, Massachusetts, who wrote his report on November 23, 1929. Messler stated that when he examined his patient before her visit to the grave, "she was able to hobble about but very little on crutches and was unable to place her foot on the ground because of severe pain. Passive motion of the foot was productive of intense pain." When he examined her on November 23, 1929, he found a foot "which moves easily in all directions without causing pain and which shows normal reactions of sensitivity to stimuli." Messler also confirmed that "the original condition was a severe dislocation of the right ankle with severe tearing and internal bleeding of the tendons and nerves."[164]

The second statement was from Dr. B. A. Godvin of Boston, written on January 20, 1930. When he examined his patient on November

2, 1929, (only two days before she visited the Power grave) he noted that there was "considerable swelling throughout the whole foot and ankle extending up the leg. There was marked limitation of all the motions of her ankle and up to this time she had never attempted to put her weight on the foot." Although he noted some swelling when he examined her again on January 19, 1930, Godvin said that his patient "was able to walk around the room without any limp."[165]

Remember that Chaput stated in his report that the Arlington woman "is now able to walk with a slight limp and the ankle is just a trifle swollen." With the above facts in mind, there are two obvious problems with this official analysis. First, the initial part of his statement is patently false. As was stated above, Dr. Godvin observed swelling, but saw no limp. Dr. Messler did not report a limp either, or any swelling. Second, to state that the ankle still had slight swelling clearly undermines, and takes out of context, just how far this woman had come in her convalescence, and the fact that after the cemetery visit, the foot could "move easily in all directions," an action which was impossible just two days before her Malden trip.

This is perhaps an example of how, at the time, the diocese seemed to want to downplay the Power miracles, in this case at the expense of the truth. Another example might be the Madeline MacFarlane case, the final entry of category number three. As we saw above, Superintendent Walsh notified the diocese that he had in his possession an affidavit from a doctor which supported this miraculous healing. Why then was this case not a category one case since it had the supporting medical testimony? Furthermore, why is this testimony by the MacFarlane family doctor not mentioned by Chaput, even if to simply discount it? This example and the one examined above make us wonder where the other skeletons are in this report. We unfortunately lack more primary sources relating to the official 35 cases to find out. Nevertheless we are thankful for the survival of these two examples to demonstrate a palpable reluctance on the part of the diocese to overstate what they felt had (or had not) taken place at Holy Cross Cemetery.

Some qualifying points should be made though about these criticisms of the report. First, we must understand the context during which it was composed. It was likely written under a great deal of internal and external pressure. The diocese wanted to know as soon as possible whether or not there was any truth to the Malden events. With this in mind, a brief overview of events, obtained within months, not years of research was just what was wanted and needed. Also, the report should be credited with not making a definite judgment as to the truth of any of the miracles it investigated. Chaput merely laid out the information at his disposal and then stated in conclusion that it "seems as though" there was one fairly reliable miracle out of all that were looked into. Concrete verdicts were withheld, perhaps explaining why the diocese has appropriately never issued an official statement on the matter. To be sure, an attitude of skepticism is the right approach when dealing with the area of the paranormal, and for that the report should be commended. In fact, a skeptical point of view is the only appropriate way to begin when delving into arenas not readily explained by science. Fortunately for us, the chancery report was not the end of these stories that lacked for scientific explanation. Scores of letters poured into the diocese's headquarters in Brighton, detailing how Father Power had apparently miraculously changed the lives of countless men and women. We now have the chance to examine some of these in full detail as well.

Chapter Five: Letters of the Impossible

Why did they do it? Why did people write to the chancery of the Archdiocese of Boston, literally from around the world, to claim that they had been healed by a priest who had been buried for generations? The letter writers certainly had no real hope for fame, no chance for publication of their claims, no point in contributing towards a cause for sainthood which never materialized. The archdiocese did not openly solicit these handwritten missives, nor in the vast majority of cases even acknowledge that they had received them. And yet they came, day after day, some running longer than ten pages, detailing heart wrenching tales of hope lost, and then regained. Most seem written out of some esoteric sense of obligation and thanksgiving, or an inner desire to make logical and linear an event which defied their own personal understanding. There is also a genuine sense of catharsis which runs throughout nearly all of these letters, often making them seem repetitious when viewed as a single body of research. Nevertheless, it is only through such repetition that we can truly gain an understanding of just how many people claimed to be healed by this man whom they had never met. In fact, the collective weight of these missives provides us with perhaps the single greatest source of materials (as yet unpublished) which document the alleged miracles attributed to the intercession of Father Patrick Power.

These letters are a treasure trove of primary sources, first hand documents written by the very people who claimed to be touched by a miracle, or the very people nearest to the case. In historical research we cannot get any closer to the supernatural. It is right here in their words. Some letters have been culled from the pile however due to their lackluster content. Accounts of jobs recovered, religious conversions achieved, and simple aches and pains eased obviously do not rise to the level of the miraculous. That still leaves us though with an ample supply of tales which simply defy scientific understanding. The level of sincerity of the letter writers is left for the reader to judge, but there seems to be no shortage of faith on the other end of these joyfully penned tales of the impossible.

Like the Archdiocese final report, we will first take a look at a letter which was accompanied by testimony from physicians. On June 19, 1930, the cardinal's brother, E. J. O'Connell, Superintendent of Cemeteries at Holy Cross Cemetery, forwarded to the archbishop's office in Brighton a communication he recently received from a Cranston, Rhode Island, woman who claimed to be "completely cured" of gallstones and cholecystitis, a gall bladder disease. "The visit to Father Power's grave being made on Nov. 24, 1929, Sunday, at nine (9) a.m., and at six thirty (6:30) p.m. the following day I received the miracle," she wrote. "It was ten (10) years that these ailments were bothering me and no doctor could cure them." She included in her mailing two letters from her physicians. Dr. A. Fridanza of Providence, Rhode Island, certified that his patient had endured "repeated attacks of cholecystitis," and Dr. G. W. Bellano also from Providence, wrote that he had diagnosed gallstones in his patient. There is no record that the diocese looked into this case in any further, a decision perhaps based on the fact that Dr. Bellano wrote in his report that "no definite diagnosis had been made" regarding this woman, other than the gallstones. Nevertheless, the Rhode Island woman wrote that she gave "great thanks to Fr. Patrick Power for his power to perform this great miracle."[166]

Although the rest of the letters are not accompanied by medical testimony, they are not necessarily any less credible than the one above. Since letters were unsolicited, there really was no point for the authors to submit and gather physician testimony anyway. Most people seemed to feel that a simple letter to inform the diocese of the event was sufficient.

A grateful mother from Dorchester, Massachusetts, wrote to the chancery on November 25, 1929, to detail the recovery of her son. "He took sick with infantile paralysis in September and couldn't even sit up with the pains in his spine, and both legs hurt him if you even touched them until the day I took him to Father Power's grave," she wrote. "I laid him down and prayed for him to be helped and to my surprise, thanks to God, he could sit up all alone...then he stood straight up...He has improved ever since."[167]

The following month another mother whose son had been the victim of infantile paralysis wrote to the archdiocese. The boy could not walk, nor "sit up without support and had to hold his head in one position. I took him over to Holy Cross Cemetery, Malden, and laid him on Father Power's grave. I started to pray and in a few minutes he sat up himself and asked me to let him stand up," she wrote on December 16, 1929. This he did, and then proceeded to walk three steps without assistance. "Then a cameraman asked him to walk toward him and he again took two or three steps...He can also move his head perfectly without suffering any pain...After I visited the grave I took him to the hospital and the doctors noticed the change immediately."[168]

Leprosy was the subject of the final letter we have from December 1929. This one arrived from Havana, Cuba, and was written entirely in Spanish by a nun who worked as a nurse at the Hospital San Lazaro. She wrote directly to Cardinal O'Connell "to communicate to your

Eminence the following miraculous case obtained through the intercession of Father Patrick Power." She wrote of a 34 year old man who for six years "has been in this department suffering from leprosy in addition to neuritis" with only "injections of morphine to somewhat mitigate the pain." The man "reached such a point of despair that in May he tried to commit suicide by using a knife to stab himself in the neck to the point of death," she wrote on December 29. At the time of the suicide attempt the nursing staff then discovered that the man's body was completely covered in sores from his feet to his head. In the middle of November 1929 he experienced three straight days of vomiting blood.

It was shortly after this that the nun noticed an article in her local newspaper that reported on the miracles attributed to Father Power that were going on that month in Malden. "It occurred to me to ask for this poor man to be converted and to be filled with faith," she said. With this in mind, she then joined with all of the sick people in the hospital to pray the Rosary, "as is the custom," and then recite the Our Father, Hail Mary, and Glory Be. However, this time she added "three prayers to Father Power to plead for us." It was not long before the leper called the sister to tell her that he wanted to immediately confess his "full repentance" to the hospital chaplain. This he did on November 19. The following day he was given the Last Rites, the Catholic sacrament reserved for those on the very brink of death, an indication not only of how close he was to dying, but also of how unlikely it would be for him to recover. "By November 22 he was completely healed of the ulcers that he had, and the pain had disappeared totally. I am very happy and thankful to Patrick Power for the miracle." The nun then added in the letter her desire that the others in the hospital might also be healed. "And I hope your Eminence that in a short while P. Power completes the work that so happily began in curing the leper from more years of suffering. I humbly ask your Eminence to send me some relic of this priest even if it is just a photograph."[169]

Perhaps because the letter came from another county, or perhaps because the case was so graphically detailed and unusual, the archdiocese decided to send an official response to the nun at the Hospital San Lazaro, one of the few times they responded to any Power-related correspondence. "His Eminence says that he learned of the case with great satisfaction and that he thanks God who has manifested His infinite Power,"[170] read a letter from the chancery dated January 15, 1930.

Did Father Power continue to heal people at the hospital, as the sister had hoped and prayed? There is some evidence that he may have, but there is a frustrating lack of details. On April 17, 1930, the diocese received another letter, this one scribed in English, again from the Hospital San Lazaro in Havana, Cuba. This time though the note was written directly by a patient, to be sure though, a different man than the subject of the letter discussed above. (Since the name of the man in this second letter, and the name of the leper in the above story have never been published, we have left out their identities for privacy reasons.) "Through the intercession of Rev. Patrick Power, I wish to state that I have obtained a great favor, I may say a miracle," this man wrote to Cardinal O'Connell. "And I do hope that this statement will be a step forward to help in the santification (sic) of the Rev. Patrick Power in whom I have great faith."[171] Unfortunately, the man provided no details of what his alleged "miracle" was, and we are left without any further correspondence from this mysterious Cuban hospital.

The next case we have came from a familiar source, the Superintendent of Cemeteries at Holy Cross, E. J. Connell, who forwarded on February 25, 1930, a story that was reported at his office. The apparent cure involved a ten month old infant from Waltham who had been the victim of a "serious skin disease, his face was covered with malignant sores and was unable to get any relief from doctors." According to O'Connell, during November 1929 "an uncle secured some earth from the grave of Father Power and after applying it constantly for a short time the child was entirely cured. The parents feel the cure was miraculous."[172] That was the extent of the details given by the superintendent.

Many more details though were included in the description of the following alleged miracle, but when examining it, some may not consider it to be all that remarkable. It is quite possible that the individual in question may have recovered anyway, not to mention the fact that her convalescence was gradual. In other words, the alleged healing did not happen immediately after the miraculous intervention was attempted. However, this brings up a larger point to consider for this and other cases of the same kind. Is a miracle only a miracle if it happens instantaneously? Can we still attribute miraculous intervention if a recovery happens days or weeks later? Obviously it is a question that is difficult to answer, especially without supporting documentation, as it is in this case. If a recovery happens days and/or weeks later the situation gets murky. What happened in that intervening time? Was there medical treatment applied which may have played a role in the healing? Did the attempt at divine intervention take place at a point when the patient was just beginning to recover naturally, with the body on the way to full health anyway, making it seem as though there was a supernatural explanation when none should have been considered?

To be clear, the Catechism of the Catholic Church defines a miracle as "a sign or wonder, such as a healing or the control of nature, which can only be attributed to divine power."[173] There is no mention of a time frame to fit the definition of an "official" miracle. In the final analysis though we may be faced with the realization that an alleged delayed miracle does not necessarily "disqualify" it, but it should raise some eyebrows. However, if we are to believe the author of the following letter, the medical personnel involved considered it to be a miracle.

Therefore we will lay out the case as usual and leave it for the reader to be the judge.

"I wish to report to you regarding the illness of my 8 year old daughter and what we consider her miraculous recovery. She was taken ill about five weeks ago," wrote a father from Arlington, Massachusetts, on April 29, 1930. The girl was diagnosed as having measles, and double lobar (in both lungs) pneumonia. Interestingly, this latter ailment is likely the same disease that struck down Father Power himself. "She has been very frail since birth and weighed only 42 pounds when taken ill. A day and a night nurse assisted the doctor who announced that her condition was so grave that she had practically no chance of survival." On March 30, 1930, she "reached a point of extreme weakness" so the family decided to employ "the use of a small bottle of water from the grave of Rev. Fr. Power at Malden, and also some of the earth," the father wrote. "After placing some of this on her we prayed and from that moment she seemed to hold her strength. We've done this daily thereafter." After 15 days the girl "passed the crisis successfully and is now convalescing. The nurses declare it's a miracle. The doctor, a very efficient and experienced practitioner of Arlington, says that he never knew anyone to recover as she did."[174]

The time frame involved was just the opposite for a cardiac asthma sufferer who wrote to the chancery from Detroit, Michigan, to make known what he called his "wonderful and instantaneous cure." He had been under a doctor's care for six months, "unable to sleep for more than one hour through the night, and frequently no sleep at all, gasping for breath through phlegm accumulations. I suffered dreadful agonies. My sister-in-law made a pilgrimage to Power's grave in…Malden and returning to Boston she forwarded me a small box of consecrated clay," he wrote on September 6, 1930, just under a year after this visit to the grave must have been made. "I received it in due course and when I lay down to sleep that night I touched my throat and praying to our Savior and Father Power asked for a cure. It was instantaneous. I fell asleep and slept continuously for ten hours, awaking much refreshed." The man then stated that he never lost a night's sleep since then, and was able to return to his job where he began working steadily ever since.

With his own apparent success, this Detroit man then decided to give some of the soil to a friend who "suffered pains in one of his legs each time he lay down. He told me from the moment it touched the afflicted limb the pain disappeared and he has had no recurrence of it." The man then offered to provide references if needed.[175]

A man from Joliet, Illinois, made the journey to Malden in November 1929 as a last resort to cure his excruciating arthritis. He apparently met with success. The following month on December 7 he wrote to Cardinal O'Connell to tell him "that I am walking everyday without my crutches and am feeling better in every way. The reason I didn't write before was because I wanted to be sure I could leave my crutches for good," he wrote. "I am so happy to know I can walk again…I have every proof you can ask for that I was a hopeless case."[176]

However, that was not the last that the diocese heard of this case. Seventeen months later this same man's wife wrote to the chancery to inform them that her husband was still doing well. "My husband was cured at Father Power's grave one year and one half ago. He had deforming arthritis in nearly every joint in his body," she wrote on May 16, 1931. "Doctors told him he wouldn't live but just a few months more at most. He had this ailment for seven years. After visiting the grave he walked without arthritis, and has walked without it ever since. When he left for Malden he weighed 98 pounds. Today he weighs 150."[177]

As with the earlier case from Havana, not just lay people wrote of their Father Power tales to the diocese. The ordained also had their stories to tell as well. "In fulfillment of a promise that I made, I am writing to inform you of a cure wrought through the intercession of Father Power," wrote a sister from St. Luke's Convent in New York City. She described an incident which happened to her 78 year old aunt in 1929. The aunt had developed dangerous gangrene in her left foot. "It spread to the knee in the direction of the heart. A consultation was called and the doctors agreed that the end was inevitable. The patient was obliged to be kept under morphine because of the intensity of the pain. The condition existed from August 1929 to May 1930," she wrote on August 12, 1931. "When the advance of the disease was at its height and all medical assistance was past, we had recourse to prayer alone and Father Power especially was invoked. Sand from the grave of Father Power was put in a small vial and then filled with Holy Water." The water was then applied to the infected areas, and a change in her condition was "wrought immediately…The spread of the disease ceased. The whole foot and places where the toe had dropped off healed over completely, and no trace of the illness whatsoever remained. The patient is up and about now for some time."[178]

As late as July 26, 1938, a woman from Meriden, Connecticut felt "duty bound to tell you of what we consider a miraculous cure through the intercession of Father Power." The actual means through which this alleged miracle took place are especially unusual. "For a number of years my husband suffered from ulcers of the stomach, consulting doctors and specialists with little or no results," she wrote. Her husband's desperation may have led him to do the following action, which some might view as a bit extreme. "About four years ago he drank a small portion of the soil (from the grave) in water, and shortly after he was relieved, and he has never had any pain or doctoring since." For good measure the wife included the names of several personal friends whom she said could vouch for the story.[179]

In an undated letter from Philadelphia, Pennsylvania, a thankful mother wrote to Cardinal O'Connell to tell him about her eleven year old son "who until last November was subject to epileptic fits of the worst kind. We commenced praying to Father Power that he would please ask God to let him not have them anymore." After a visit to the grave the episodes stopped. The woman enclosed a $100 check to the archdiocese in thanksgiving and noted that "I have some of the clay for his grave which my boy now wears."[180]

In another undated letter, "a client of Father Power" who wished to remain nameless wrote of the end of a lengthy illness. "I had been ill for some years and was under the care of the best doctors that could be secured. I got very little relief and it was the opinion of many that I would never get well." An "unusual affection and devotion" then began to develop on the part of this "client" towards Father Power. "I started a novena in his honor and on the ninth day I started to improve and have been getting steadily better ever since. I was also cured of dizzy spells after praying to Father Power."[181]

When we look at the collective weight of these letters, Father Power had apparently interceded to cure people of gallstones, gall bladder disease, useless limbs, paralysis, measles, pneumonia, epilepsy, cardiac asthma, deforming arthritis, gangrene, ulcers, and even skin diseases such as leprosy. In chapter one, we noted the parallels between Father Patrick Power's life and the life of another known miracle worker born in the same generation, Father Nelson Baker. Interestingly, we not only have biographical parallels between the two men, but we can also now point out parallels in their miraculous work. Both men had, and still have, people praying to them for their miraculous intercession long after their deaths. Not only that, cures of useless limbs, paralysis, epilepsy, and various skin diseases show up frequently in the repertoire of both men. To be sure the parallels should not be overstated but when you consider how rare actual miraculous ability is, and how unexplained is its scientific genesis, any parallels in its select club of practitioners is useful in our quest for understanding. Consider also that miracles attributed to Father Power and miracles attributed to Father Baker were taking place at roughly the same time in the northeastern United States. Nelson Baker's miraculous work began in the late 1800s/early1900s, and apparently continue to this day. The same can be said for Patrick Power if we are to believe the Walsh report from chapter two which stated that miracles relating to the Power grave may go back at least 30 years before the events of 1929, not to mention any miracles which may happened during Power's life.

This of course raises another question. Do people still pray to Father Power to ask for his intercession? One way to answer that question is to visit the grave of Patrick Power today and see all of the artifacts left at the fence which protects the marble slab over his remains. At a visit in May 2005, no less than 240 different objects could be counted along the ground and among the iron posts. Anonymous souls had left all sorts of trinkets and mementos. Here is a complete list.

- 145 rosaries
- 12 palm branches
- 10 handwritten notes
- 9 floral garlands
- 8 chains with a cross
- 7 photographs
- 6 holy cards
- 5 religious statues
- 4 angel pins
- 3 key chains
- 2 beaded bracelets
- 2 handmade angels
- 2 images of Jesus
- 2 scapulas
- 2 stuffed animals
- 2 yellow floral necklaces
- 1 American flag
- 1 angel doll
- 1 bag with a bow
- 1 basket of flowers
- 1 bronze medal
- 1 business card
- 1 Easter basket
- 1 hair tie
- 1 handmade floral cross
- 1 handmade palm cross
- 1 heart shaped plaque
- 1 Padre Pio photo
- 1 Pope John Paul II photo
- 1 potted plant
- 1 prayer booklet
- 1 prayer to St. Raphael
- 1 ribbon
- 1 Santa Claus hat
- 1 yarn bracelet
- Countless pennies, nickels, dimes, quarters, half dollars, and dollar coins were strewn over the marble slab, and on the dirt surrounding the grave as well.[182]

According to Richard Bradley, Director of Operations for the Catholic Cemetery Association of the Archdiocese of Boston at Holy Cross Cemetery, every week the area around the Power grave needs to be cleared of new artifacts that accumulate there, and every Thursday afternoon a prayer group gathers to sing and pray at the spot. These facts perhaps more than any others demonstrate the continued appeal of praying to Father Power, and according to Bradley, Power's notoriety is still not just a local phenomenon. In the early 1990s, there was a Catholic conference in Boston where priests and monsignors came to visit from all over the world. Local sightseeing was on the agenda and "on the schedule was to drive through Holy Cross Cemetery. The tour buses would come through and this one tour bus stopped. I happened to be out there and an old Irish priest gets off the bus and wants to see where Father Power's grave is," said Bradley. "So I showed him and one of the things that he told me was that there was a nursery rhyme for the school kids back in Ireland about Father Power. He's a big deal back in Ireland."[183] The song in question probably is "O Father Power of Holy Cross," composed by Edward L. Sullivan, published by C. I. Hicks Music Company of Boston in 1929.[184]

> O Father Power of Holy Cross/Hearken to they Pilgrims' plea/Pray our God that in His Might/He, our earthly woes relieve./O Father Power of Holy Cross/At thy shrine on bended knee/We God's children seeking aid/Place our heavenly hopes in thee./O Father Power of Holy Cross/Thou, thru who God's blessings yield/ Hear, oh hear the Pilgrims' plea/Lord, my God! that I be healed.

(Refrain)
Saintly priest, oh hear our prayer/Friend of God, His works
declare,/O Father Power, so meek and just,/In thy mercy pray
for us.[185]

Although perhaps not a masterpiece, this hymn and the preceding
story testify to Power's enduring appeal. However, as the number of
people who actually witnessed the events at Malden become fewer and
fewer, the appeal and memory of Patrick Power might fade. It will then
be left to a new generation to rediscover this enigmatic priest and his
mysterious earthly remains. Perhaps then a new chapter to his ongoing
story can be written.

Here we have at least laid the groundwork to begin to address some
fundamental questions about this man, questions posed at the outset.
Was Patrick Power a miracle worker during his lifetime? We uncovered a great deal of circumstantial evidence to try to answer this basic
query, including his lineage, birthday, death day, writings, pilgrimages,
and bouts of suffering. We also pointed out that if Power was a wonder worker in his own lifetime this would explain why local residents
singled out his grave for divine help long before the events of 1929
made him famous. Are these answers definitive? Admittedly no, but
few things in the paranormal are, particularly when relevant primary
sources are so scarce. However, the collective weight of this evidence

does at least suggest that Power may have been more than just Power by name, as his fellow seminarian said in the early 1860s.

Were the events at Malden in 1929 true miracles? As was stated at the outset, the reader will have to answer that one on their own. However, we have attempted to assist the reader in this endeavor by laying out the facts as objectively as possible from chancery reports, letters, inquiries, and private correspondence sent to the archdiocese. In the final analysis, although we may not be able to give a concrete answer to either of these basic questions, we cannot deny the fact that the people who were allegedly healed by Patrick Power insisted that they were telling the truth. Their level of sincerity is certainly palpable in numerous letters and interviews. Not only that, the investigations into the miracles were conducted by some of the most renowned priests in the diocese at the time, all of whom staked their reputations on their reports.

Yet even if we somehow could come to a place in our minds where we felt comfortable in conclusively answering the above two questions, we are still left with another more basic deficiency in our understanding. Why Patrick Power? How could it be possible that a poor, obscure, immigrant parish priest, who never made it a day past the age of 25, be a miracle worker? Then again, I seem to recall another poor, obscure young man who many people considered to be quite a gifted miracle worker during his life, and apparently still is to this day, long after his death. Perhaps one day He can give us some answers.

Appendix: The Miraculous Roster

A victim of infantile paralysis, 4 year-old Daniel Bellino of Worcester, MA, walked for the first time without the aid of braces after his visit to the Power grave.
International Newsreel courtesy of Archdiocese of Boston Archives

A selected list of documented miracles attributed to the intercession of Father Patrick Power printed in media reports. When known, the name, age, hometown, likely date of the miracle, and a brief description of the alleged cure as it was reported, are included.

Aboudt, Joseph, Boston, November 9, 1929. Pain disappeared in his fractured wrist subsequent to his visit to the tomb.[186]

Barry, Edna, 24, West Medford, Massachusetts, November 12, 1929. Water from Power's grave ended Barry's debilitating arthritis which had confined her to a hospital bed for months.[187]

Bellino, Daniel, 4, Worcester, Massachusetts, November 1929. A victim of infantile paralysis since birth, he walked without the aid of his braces following his trip to the shrine.[188]

Boulmer, Doris, 4, Northbridge, Massachusetts, November 12, 1929. Although she never walked since birth, Boulmer was placed on top of Power's tombstone and then walked without aid.[189]

Bourdon, Natalie, 20 months old, Watertown, Massachusetts, November 16, 1929. Partially blind since birth, Bourdon completely recovered her eyesight during her trip to Holy Cross Cemetery.[190]

Braley, John, 5, Providence, Rhode Island, November 12, 1929. Paralyzed since birth, Braley walked subsequent to kneeling in front of the shrine.[191]

Brothers, Irene, 9, East Boston, November 9, 1929. After five years of being unable to walk, she began to do so immediately after praying at the grave.[192]

Budkevechus, Frances, Brockton, Massachusetts, November 10, 1929. Reported improvement in paralysis while at the burial site.[193]

Camera, James, 42, Sanford, Maine, November 11, 1929. Walked without crutches for the first time since the age of four immediately following his few minutes of prayer in front of Power's tombstone.[194]

Canzona, Louis, 8, South Boston, November 11, 1929. Reported improvement in infantile paralysis after a visit to the shrine.[195]

Chollette, Rita, 7, Manchester, New Hampshire, November 10, 1929. Crippled at birth, Chollette regained the use of all limbs following her anointment with water from Power's tombstone.[196]

Costello, Ralph, South Boston, November 12, 1929. Although his right arm had been paralyzed since the age of four, Costello raised his arm as he stood in front of Power's grave.[197]

Cotter, Frank, 15, South Boston. Infantile paralysis had given him a limp since the age of four, but subsequent to praying at the gravesite the limp disappeared.[198]

Coughlin, Florence, 19, Malden, Massachusetts, November 9, 1929. Coughlin wore a brace around her leg for years, but walked freely without the use of the brace after visiting the cemetery.[199]

Cronin, James, Saugus, Massachusetts, November 5, 1929. Cured of partial blindness subsequent to visiting the grave.[200]

Cunningham, Raphael Mrs., Everett, Massachusetts, November 1929. Cured of rheumatism following a trip to the Power shrine.[201]

Curley, Catherine, 50, Roxbury, Massachusetts, November 16, 1929. Recovered movement in her arm after six years of rigidity during her trip to Holy Cross.[202]

Dancheta, Charles, 10, Lawrence, Massachusetts, November 12, 1929. Suffered paralysis in one of his legs since birth, but walked away without assistance after kneeling in prayer at the burial site.[203]

De Luca, Josephine, 5, Lawrence, Massachusetts, November 16, 1929. Walked for the first time without braces following her time at the gravesite.[204]

De Mower, Alfred, 6, Lawrence, Massachusetts, November 9, 1929. This boy had been unable to walk for two years, but walked unassisted after praying with his parents at the cemetery.[205]

De Muso, Torilli, 21, Revere, Massachusetts, November 9, 1929. For several years her left arm had been paralyzed. She was able to raise it after her time at the gravesite.[206]

Del Russo, Nicholas, 15, East Boston, November 8, 1929. Unable to talk since birth, Del Russo began to speak after he kissed Power's tombstone.[207]

Des Rochess, Alice, 23, Manchester, New Hampshire, November 11, 1929. Reported improvement in paralysis after visiting the shrine.[208] She lost the use of her limbs after nearly drowning five years prior. She was carried into the cemetery in the arms of relatives, and then apparently walked unaided after praying in front of the grave marker.[209]

Fitzgerald, Arthur, Malden, Massachusetts, November 5, 1929. Paralyzed from the waist down, but after paying a visit to the cemetery he began to walk for the first time in his life.[210]

Gallagher, Doris, 22, Holyoke, Massachusetts, November 12, 1929. Following a few moments of prayer at the gravesite, Gallagher walked away easily despite 14 years with a stiff and crippled leg.[211]

Galloway, John, 24, Grinnel, Iowa, November 16, 1929. Injured in a car accident in 1928, Galloway stated that the leg injured in the crash had healed subsequent to praying at the burial site.[212]

Goldberg, Morris, 14, Dorchester, Massachusetts, November 11, 1929. Walked with crutches for eight years until visiting the grave, after which he walked unaided and left his crutches at All Souls' Chapel.[213]

Josephine LeBlanc of Woburn, MA, who walked unassisted without the aid of her cane or crutches after praying at the Power burial site.

International Newsreel courtesy of Archdiocese of Boston Archives

Gonsalves, Ayres, 5, Woburn, Massachusetts, November 12, 1929. Previously this boy had been unable to stand or to grasp objects in his hands, but was able to do both during his visit to Power's grave.[214]

Graul, William, 6, South Boston, November 1929. Brought to Boston City Hospital near death with a contracted throat and breathing trouble. Water brought from Power's grave opened the throat and saved his life.[215]

Hunt, Helen, 22, Danbury, Connecticut, November 10, 1929. Paralyzed for twelve years, she walked unaided subsequent to praying at the shrine.[216]

Iuradi, Francis, 11, West Bewton, Massachusetts, November 9, 1929. Could not walk for several years but walked with minimal assistance after praying at the burial site.[217]

Keating, Robert, 30, East Boston, November 17, 1929. Unable to walk due to infantile paralysis, he walked unassisted after praying at the gravesite.[218]

La Flamme, Claire, 19, Lowell, Massachusetts, November 17, 1929. Unable to walk due to infantile paralysis, she walked unassisted after kneeling and praying in front of the grave.[219]

LeBlanc, Josephine, Woburn, Massachusetts, November 22, 1929. Able to walk without cane or crutches after visit to the cemetery.[220]

Leguro, Vincent Mrs., Allston, Massachusetts, November 12, 1929. Crippled for four years, Leguro walked away from the shrine following a few moments of prayer.[221]

Lentell, John, 16, Roxbury, Massachusetts, November 16, 1929. Reported improvement in his paralysis after his time at the burial site.[222]

MacFarlane, Madeline, 9, Chelsea, Massachusetts, November 9, 1929. Cured of paralysis during her time at the cemetery.[223]

Madden, Thomas, 12, Providence, Rhode Island, November 12, 1929. Reported improvement in his ability to walk following his pilgrimage to Malden.[224]

Matzie, Cecelia, 9, Boston, November 1929. Unable to walk since the age of four when she was crippled with infantile paralysis, Matzie began to walk unassisted subsequent to her visit to the cemetery.[225]

McMahon, Francis, 12, Somerville, Massachusetts, November 11, 1929. Nearly blind for several years, the boy recovered his eyesight and exclaimed to his mother, "I can see the crowd of people" after praying near the remains of Father Power.[226]

Meaney, Daniel, Malden, Massachusetts, November 16, 1929. Reported that his eyesight had improved so much that he was able to leave his glasses at the cemetery.[227]

Moody, Laura, 18, Dorchester, Massachusetts, November 12, 1929. Cured of paralyzing spinal arthritis after her visit to the grave.[228]

O'Hearn, Mary, Everett, Massachusetts, August 1929. Although physicians told her that she would be permanently deaf after losing her hearing in May, 1929, O'Hearn regained her hearing after her third visit to Power's gravesite in August 1929.[229]

O'Neill, Vincent, 7, Somerville, Massachusetts, November 11, 1929. Blind since birth, but when brought to All Soul's Chapel after being at the burial site said, "I can see pictures."[230]

Panora, James, 6, Revere, Massachusetts, November 4, 1929. A deaf-mute for years, Panora was brought to the gravesite by his mother and then began to speak to her.[231]

Pino, Ida, 13, Rockland, Massachusetts, November 12, 1929. Pino walked away from the grave after 12 years of paralysis in her legs.[232]

Reynolds, Eugene, 3, Mattapan, Massachusetts, November 12, 1929. After being brought to the shrine, Reynolds was able to walk for the first time.[233]

Rienzi, Raphael, 15, Readville, Massachusetts, November 16, 1929. Screamed while kneeling at the grave and stated that the stiffness in his leg had disappeared. Later Rienzi discarded the brace he had worn on the leg for several years.[234]

Rohowan, Nicholas, Boston, Massachusetts, November 10, 1929. Reported improvement in near blindness after praying at the Power shrine.[235]

Sadorium, Louise, West Roxbury, Massachusetts, November 12, 1929. Sadorium walked away from the gravesite without the use of her crutches.[236]

Sargent, Effie May, 3, Haverhill, Massachusetts, November 12, 1929. Although unable to walk normally for many months before her visit to Holy Cross Cemetery, Sargent began to run and walk without any problems after she was led to the burial site.[237]

Sheehan, Francis, 4, Walpole, Massachusetts, November 16, 1929. Although previously unable to walk normally, Sheehan walked without difficulty at the shrine.[238]

Sidman, Samuel, 20, Dorchester, Massachusetts, November 1929. This young man was a cripple for many years, but walked without the use of his wheelchair following his prayer session at the gravesite.[239]

Simmonovitch, Victor, 20, Boston, November 9, 1929. After many years of being unable to talk, Simmonovitch regained his speech while kneeling and praying in front of the Power tombstone.[240]

Simpson, Joseph, Newport, Rhode Island, November 12, 1929. Crippled for two years, this man walked away from the shrine without his crutches.[241]

Smith, Mary, 60, Shirley, Massachusetts, November 9, 1929. After praying at the site, she was able to raise both of her heretofore paralyzed arms over her head.[242]

Strongman, Blanche, Malden, Massachusetts, November 1929. Cured of blindness during her trip to the cemetery.[243]

Thomas, Selma, 17, Waterville, Maine, November 10, 1929. Experienced improvement in paralysis subsequent to being brought to the Power tomb.[244]

Walsh, Nicholas, 11, Roxbury, Massachusetts, November 10, 1929. Reported improvement in infantile paralysis after praying at the gravesite.[245]

Whittaker, Richard, Roxbury, Massachusetts, November 11, 1929. More than six years of arthritis ended subsequent to this World War I veteran's trip to Holy Cross Cemetery on Armistice Day, now called Veterans' Day.[246]

Williams, Ezra, Gloucester, Massachusetts, November 12, 1929. Prayers in front of Power's grave and water from the carved out chalice on the tombstone ended this woman's 26 years of not being able to walk.[247]

Zorhinas, Andrew, 5, Nashua, New Hampshire, November 11, 1929. Deaf since birth, this boy regained his hearing after two journeys to the Malden cemetery.[248]

Endnotes

[1] "Father Patrick J. Power Memorial Booklet," <u>Boston Sunday Post</u> 1 December 1929, C9, Holy Cross Cemetery Archives.

[2] Ibid.

[3] <u>Catechism of the Catholic Church</u>, 2nd. ed. (Washington, D.C.: United States Catholic Conference, 2000), 883.

[4] "Father Power Was Born and Died on 'Stainless Day,'" Power, Rev. Patrick J., M-1587, folder 1, Archdiocese of Boston Archives.

[5] "Who on Earth was the Rev. Patrick J. Power?" <u>Malden Evening News</u> 12 December 1979, and "Fr. Power, Whose Grave Is Shrine, Assistant Pastor in Chicopee in 1869," Power folder 1, Archdiocese of Boston Archives.

[6] Ibid.

[7] Bullard, F. Lauriston. "Malden – In Retrospect and Prospect." <u>Atlantic Monthly</u> October 1930, 538, Holy Cross Cemetery Archives.

[8] "Father Patrick J. Power Memorial Booklet," C5.

[9] Ibid., C6.

[10] Ibid.

[11] Laval history courtesy of the Laval University website, http://www.scom.ulaval.ca/ presentation/anglais/ background.html.

[12] "Who on Earth was the Rev. Patrick J. Power?"

[13] Ibid.

[14] "Father Patrick J. Power Memorial Booklet," C8.

[15] Ibid.

[16] "Books in Fr. Power's Writing Are Preserved at Worcester," <u>Boston Daily Globe</u> 13 November 1929, and "Fr. Power, Whose Grave Is Shrine…"

[17] "Father Power on Miracles," Power folder 1, Archdiocese of Boston Archives.

[18] Ruth Rejnis, <u>The Everything Saints Book</u> (Avon, Massachusetts: Adams Media Corporation, 2001), 197.

[19] http://www. ssadb.qc.ca. This is the official website of the Basilica of St. Anne de Beaupre.

[20] Ibid.

[21] "Father Patrick J. Power," Power folder 1, Archdiocese of Boston Archives.

[22] Floyd Anderson, <u>Apostle of Charity: The Father Nelson Henry Baker Story</u> (Lackawanna,

New York: Our Lady of Victory Homes of Charity, 2002), 44.

[23] "Father Patrick J. Power."

[24] "Father Patrick J. Power Memorial Booklet," C8.

[25] See "The Early Life of Patrick Power," Power folder 1, Archdiocese of Boston Archives, and Bullard, 538.

[26] Diocese of Albany Archives, personal interview with the author, 21 July 2005.

[27] "Children Paid for Tomb of Fr. Power," Power folder 1, Archdiocese of Boston Archives.

[28] Bullard, 538.

[29] Photostat copy in Power folder 1, Archdiocese of Boston Archives.

[30] "Children Paid for Tomb of Fr. Power."

[31] "Fr. Power, Whose Grave Is Shrine..."

[32] Power folder 6, Archdiocese of Boston Archives.

[33] Ibid.

[34] "Work Speeded Fr. Power's Death," Power folder 1, Archdiocese of Boston Archives.

[35] "Father Power on Miracles."

[36] "Children Paid for Tomb of Fr. Power."

[37] "Father Power on Miracles."

[38] Ibid.

[39] "Work Speeded Fr. Power's Death."

[40] Ibid.

[41] "Father Power on Miracles."

[42] "Father Patrick J. Power."

[43] "Eulogy Found Of Fr. Power," Power folder 1, Archdiocese of Boston Archives.

[44] The comparisons between Power and Baker do not end with suffering. Both men were multilingual, excellent singers, accomplished scholars in their seminaries, fond of children, and of Irish lineage.

[45] Malcolm Day, A Treasury of Saints (Hauppauge, New York: Barron's, 2002), 114.

[46] Ibid., 123.

[47] Ibid., 125.

[48] Bradley, Richard, personal interview with the author, 16 May 2005.

[49] "Father Patrick J. Power Memorial Booklet."

[50] J. Havelock Fidler, Earth Energy: A Dowser's Investigation of Ley Lines (Wellingborough, Northamptonshire: The Aquarian Press, 1988), 180.

[51] Ibid., 182.

[52] Cemetery history courtesy of Richard Bradley, Director of Operations, Catholic Cemetery Association of the Archdiocese of Boston at Holy Cross Cemetery in Malden, personal interview with the author, 16 May 2005.

[53] "Cure 30 Years Ago At Grave Reported," Boston Daily Globe 13 November 1929.

[54] Walsh, Joseph, report to the chancery, 1 December 1929, Power folder 7, Archdiocese of Boston Archives.

[55] Ibid.

[56] Bullard, 539.

[57] Ibid., 538.

[58] "Three Persons Tell An Amazing Story," Power folder 1, Archdiocese of Boston Archives.

[59] Walsh, Joseph, report to the chancery, 1 December 1929.

[60] "Ask the Globe," Boston Globe 22 April 1997.

[61] "Hundreds of thousands sought 'cure' at grave," Malden Evening News 10 December 1979, Power folder 1, Archdiocese of Boston Archives.

[62] "Tomb of Priest Becomes Shrine For Afflicted Folk," Boston Daily Globe 31 October 1929.

[63] "Miracle Seekers in Crush at Cemetery Shrine; Police Forced to Remove Gravestone," New York Times 11 November 1929.

[64] "Three Persons Tell An Amazing Story," Power folder 1, Archdiocese of Boston Archives.

[65] Walsh, Joseph, report to the chancery, 1 December 1929.

[66] "Scores Faint In Record Pilgrimage Of 200,000 To Shrine Of Malden Priest," Power folder 1, Archdiocese of Boston Archives.

[67] Bullard, 539.

[68] "The Grave At Malden," The Gazette 28 December 1929, Power folder 1, Archdiocese of Boston Archives. This is a reprint of the Commonweal article.

[69] "Throngs Seek Cure At Priest's Grave," New York Times 12 November 1929.

[70] Walsh, Joseph, report to the chancery, 4 December 1929, Power folder 7, Archdiocese of Boston Archives.

[71] Name published in "Hundreds of thousands sought 'cure' at grave."

[72] Walsh, Joseph, report to the chancery, 1 December 1929.

[73] Walsh, Joseph, report to the chancery, 4 December 1929.

[74] "The Grave At Malden."

[75] Ibid.

[76] Ibid.

[77] "Cardinal Visits Malden Shrine," Boston Daily Globe 13 November 1929.

[78] "Cardinal At Shrine Again," Boston Sunday Post 17 November 1929, Power folder 1, Archdiocese of Boston Archives.

[79] Walsh, Joseph, report to the chancery, 1 December 1929.

[80] "Crowd At Shrine Damages Tablet," Boston Daily Globe 11 November 1929.

[81] "Wonders at the grave, Malden flooded by hopefuls," Malden Evening News 11 December 1979, Holy Cross Cemetery Archives.

[82] "Scores Faint In Record Pilgrimage…"

[83] "Throngs Seek Cure At Priest's Grave."

[84] "High Prelate Joins Pilgrims At Shrine," Rutland Herald 13 November 1929, Power folder 1, Archdiocese of Boston Archives.

[85] "Scores Faint In Record Pilgrimage…"

[86] Ibid.

[87] Bradley, Richard, personal interview with the author, 16 May 2005.

[88] During my research for the book The Mysteries of Father Baker (Western New York Wares, 2005), and even after the book came out, there were many people who told me of certain miracles attributed to Baker that had happened to them or to members of their family, but they did not want the story to be published. The reasons given were twofold. First, these individuals sought no public recognition for what had happened. They considered the matter a private one between them and God. Second, some doubted that people would believe the story anyway. Thus with the area of miracles, one always has to assume that there is a likelihood that there are more people who may have been miraculously touched, but have chosen to remain anonymous. We can assume that this is a strong possibility with the Power miracles, considering the fact that nearly a million people visited the grave that autumn.

[89] "200,000 Are Drawn To Malden 'Shrine,'" The New York Times 18 November 1929.

[90] "Scores Faint In Record Pilgrimage…"

[91] "Miracles: fact or fantasy?" Malden Evening News 14 December 1979, Holy Cross Cemetery Archives.

[92] "Aura of Faith Surrounds Shrine," Power folder 1, Archdiocese of Boston Archives.

[93] "The grave in the Holy Cross Cemetery," Neponset Valley Daily News 29 November 1929, Power folder 1, Archdiocese of Boston Archives.

[94] Ibid.

[95] "Miracles: fact or fantasy?"

[96] "Throngs Seek Cure At Priest's Grave," and "200,000 Are Drawn To Malden 'Shrine.'"

[97] "200,000 Pilgrims Visit," Power folder 1, Archdiocese of Boston Archives.

[98] "Malden Cemetery to Be Closed to Pilgrims; Cardinal O'Connell Will Investigate 'Cures,'" New York Times 23 November 1929.

[99] Bradley, Richard, personal interview with the author, 16 May 2005.

[100] Bullard, 545.

[101] Power folder 3, Archdiocese of Boston Archives.

[102] Ibid., Power folder 2.

[103] Ibid.

[104] Ibid., Power folder 4.

[105] Ibid., Power folder 2.

[106] Ibid., Power folder 4.

[107] Ibid.

[108] Ibid., Power folder 2.

[109] Ibid.

[110] Ibid.

[111] Ibid.

[112] Ibid.

[113] For more proof of this see The Mysteries of Father Baker, "The Corning Miracles," and "The Victorian Miracles." In Nelson Baker's case he also demonstrated his miraculous ability in Corning, New York, not just the Buffalo area. "The Victorian Miracles" demonstrates that people reported their alleged miracles attributed to Baker during his life, and after his death, from a variety of different geographical locations around the country.

[114] Power folder 6, Archdiocese of Boston Archives.

[115] Ibid., Power folder 8.

[116] "Father Power's Body Is Moved To A New Tomb," Power folder 1, Archdiocese of Boston Archives.

[117] Ibid.

[118] Bradley, Richard, personal interview with the author, 16 May 2005.

[119] Ibid.

[120] Rejnis, 101.

[121] "Move Body Of The Rev. Fr. Power," Power folder 1, Archdiocese of Boston Archives.

[122] "Father Power's Body Is Moved To A New Tomb."

[123] "Move Body Of The Rev. Fr. Power."

[124] "Father Power's Body Is Moved To A New Tomb."

[125] "Shrine Cemetery Open New Year's," Power folder 1, Archdiocese of Boston Archives.

[126] "Wonders at the grave…"

[127] "Thousands at Malden Grave," Power folder 1, Archdiocese of Boston Archives.

[128] "5000 Pilgrims Visit Grave of Fr. Power," Power folder 1, Archdiocese of Boston Archives.

[129] "Wonders at the grave…"

[130] Archdiocese of Boston Archives, Power folder 5.

[131] Ibid.

[132] Ibid., Power folder 6.

[133] Ibid., Power folder 7.

[134] Ibid., Power folder 5.

[135] Ibid.

[136] Ibid.

[137] Ibid.

[138] "Throngs Again At Shrine More Cures Reported," Boston Daily Globe 12 November

1929.

[139] Ibid.

[140] Ibid., Power folder 6.

[141] Ibid.

[142] All of the Grattan Kerans account is from "Most Noted Cure at Malden," Catholic Record 26 December 1929, Power folder 1, Archdiocese of Boston Archives.

[143] "Miracle at Holy Cross Cemetery," Malden Observer 24 December 1998, Holy Cross Cemetery Archives.

[144] Name published in "10 Cures In Day At Malden Grave," Boston Daily Globe 11 November 1929.

[145] Power folder 5, Archdiocese of Boston Archives.

[146] Ibid., Power folder 6.

[147] Ibid., Power folder 5.

[148] Name published in "Crowd At Shrine Damages Tablet."

[149] "Miss Helen Hunt Dies From A Baffling Form Of Sleeping Sickness," 14 January 1932, Power folder 1, Archdiocese of Boston Archives.

[150] "Latest Facts About the Miracles Reported at the Malden Shrine," New York Journal 11 January 1930, Power folder 1, Archdiocese of Boston Archives.

[151] Ibid.

[152] Ibid.

[153] Power folder 5, Archdiocese of Boston Archives.

[154] Name printed in "Hundreds Pray at Shrine All Night," Boston Daily Globe 13 November 1929.

[155] Power folder 5, Archdiocese of Boston Archives.

[156] Walsh, Joseph, report to the chancery, 1 December 1929.

[157] Power folder 5, Archdiocese of Boston Archives.

[158] "Cardinal Visits Malden Shrine."

[159] Power folder 5, Archdiocese of Boston Archives.

[160] Ibid.

[161] Ibid., Power folder 7.

[162] "Hundreds Pray at Shrine All Night."

[163] Ibid.

[164] Ibid.

[165] Ibid.

[166] Ibid., Power folder 3.

[167] Ibid., Power folder 5.

[168] Ibid., Power folder 7.

[169] Ibid., Power folder 2. Letter translated by the author, and The University of Chicago Spanish Dictionary 5th ed. (Chicago, Illinois: The University of Chicago Press, 2002).

[170] Ibid., Power folder 3.

[171] Ibid., Power folder 4.

[172] Ibid., Power folder 3.

[173] Catechism of the Catholic Church, 888.

[174] Power folder 3, Archdiocese of Boston Archives.

[175] Ibid., Power folder 4.

[176] Ibid., Power folder 6.

[177] Ibid., Power folder 5.

[178] Ibid., Power folder 4. As noted, the letter describing this case was written on 12 August 1931. Two days later, a different nun from the same convent wrote a letter to Cardinal O'Connell which described a curious Father Power-related incident that had just lately

transpired. At a recent meal, the nun's father began choking. All attempts to save his life failed, except for one. His salvation was a vile of water that the man drank as a last resort. The water was from Father Power's grave.

[179] Ibid., Power folder 2.

[180] Ibid., Power folder 3.

[181] Ibid., Power folder 4. The rare mention of a novena is not surprising given that the "client" hailed from Tonawanda, a suburb of Buffalo, New York, where Father Nelson Baker had made the centuries-old practice of novenas (a nine day prayer service) quite popular in the local Catholic community in the early twentieth century.

[182] Personal visit, 16 May 2005, Holy Cross Cemetery, Malden.

[183] Bradley, Richard, personal interview with the author, 16 May 2005.

[184] "The Church: its thoughts on 'curses' (sic) then and now," Malden Evening News 13 December 1979, Holy Cross Cemetery Archives.

[185] Ibid.

[186] "10 Cures In Day At Malden Grave."

[187] "Medford Woman Aided By Water From Grave," Boston Daily Globe 13 November 1929.

[188] "Latest Facts About the Miracles…"

[189] "Scores Faint In Record Pilgrimage…"

[190] "Cardinal At Shrine Again." This girl's name was listed as "Bowden" in "Latest Facts About the Miracles…"

[191] "Scores Faint In Record Pilgrimage…"

[192] "10 Cures In Day At Malden Grave."

[193] "Crowd At Shrine Damages Tablet."

[194] "Throngs Again at Shrine More Cures Reported."

[195] Ibid.

[196] "Two At Manchester Are Reported As Improved," Boston Daily Globe 13 November 1929.

[197] "Scores Faint In Record Pilgrimage…"

[198] "Miracle at Holy Cross Cemetery."

[199] Ibid., and "10 Cures In Day At Malden Grave."

[200] "Hundreds of thousands sought 'cure' at grave."

[201] Ibid.

[202] "Cardinal At Shrine Again."

[203] "Scores Faint In Record Pilgrimage…" This boy's name was reported as "Danderta" in "Cardinal At Shrine Again."

[204] "Cardinal At Shrine Again."

[205] "10 Cures In Day At Malden Grave."

[206] Ibid.

[207] "Crowd Of 30,000 At Priest's Grave," Boston Daily Globe 9 November 1929.

[208] "Throngs Again at Shrine More Cures Reported."

[209] "Boston Cardinal at 'Miracle' Grave," New York Times 13 November 1929. The Times listed her last name as "Desrochers" and her age as 25. The Globe report and the Times report agreed on the hometown, the first name, and the type of miracle.

[210] "10 Cures In Day At Malden Grave."

[211] "Scores Faint In Record Pilgrimage…"

[212] "Cardinal At Shrine Again."

[213] "Throngs Again at Shrine More Cures Reported."

[214] "Cardinal Visits Malden Shrine."

[215] "The grave in the Holy Cross Cemetery."

[216] "Latest Facts About the Miracles…," and "Miss Helen M. Hunt Dies…," and "Crowd At Shrine Damages Tablet."

[217] "10 Cures In Day At Malden Grave."

[218] "2 More Healed At Grave," Power folder 1, Archdiocese of Boston Archives.

[219] Ibid.

[220] International Newsreel Photo credit, Archdiocese of Boston Archives, photo P2.27.

[221] "Scores Faint In Record Pilgrimage…"

[222] "Cardinal At Shrine Again."

[223] "Hundreds Pray at Shrine All Night." The chancery report stated ten years old, and the *Globe* stated nine years old. The discrepancy likely exists because the report was issued the following year, and the girl probably turned ten during that time.

[224] "Cardinal Visits Malden Shrine."

[225] "Cured at 'Miracle Grave,'" Boston Post Gazette 29 November 1929, Power folder 1, Archdiocese of Boston Archives.

[226] "10 Cures In Day At Malden Grave."

[227] "Cardinal At Shrine Again."

[228] "Throngs Again at Shrine More Cures Reported."

[229] "Three Persons Tell An Amazing Story."

[230] "Throngs Again at Shrine More Cures Reported."

[231] "The grave in the Holy Cross Cemetery."

[232] "Scores Faint In Record Pilgrimage…"

[233] "Cardinal Visits Malden Shrine."

[234] "Cardinal At Shrine Again."

[235] "Crowd At Shrine Damages Tablet."

[236] "Scores Faint In Record Pilgrimage…"

[237] Ibid.

[238] "Cardinal At Shrine Again."

[239] "Latest Facts About the Miracles…"

[240] "10 Cures In Day At Malden Grave."

[241] "Scores Faint In Record Pilgrimage…"

[242] Ibid.

[243] "Hundreds of thousands sought 'cure' at grave."

[244] "Crowd At Shrine Damages Tablet."

[245] Ibid.

[246] "Throngs Again at Shrine More Cures Reported."

[247] "Scores Faint In Record Pilgrimage…"

[248] "Nashua Parents Believe Deaf Boy Now Can Hear," Boston Daily Globe 13 November 1929.

About the Author

John Koerner is the author of *The Mysteries of Father Baker* (Western New York Wares, 2005, www.buffalobooks.com). He has an MA in American History from the State University of New York, College at Brockport, where he was an award winning graduate student writer. Koerner graduated summa cum laude from the Honors Program with a BA in Communication/Journalism from St. John Fisher College in Rochester, New York. His writing has appeared in the *Hamburg Sun*, the *Springville Journal*, and the *Next Step Magazine*. Born in Buffalo, New York, Koerner is also an accomplished historical tour guide. He has worked as an instructional guide for Rochester's Neighborhood of the Arts, Roam Buffalo, and as a founding member of Haunted History Ghost Walks, Western New York's leading paranormal research organization. Together with his wife, Tammy, he is also the co-director, and co-founder of Buffalo Literary Walking Tours, an organization dedicated to preserving two centuries of literary heritage in the Buffalo region. Koerner is also a social sciences professor at Niagara County Community College, Genesee Community College, and Erie Community College.

Printed in the United States
208444BV00001B/334/A

9 781425 990619